ABOUT MAPS

Since the world is round, the best kind of map is a round one, which we call a globe. It is not always possible to have a globe at hand, and it would require very big ones to provide maps of sections of the world as large as we may need them for careful study.

Map-makers, therefore, have tried different ways of showing the world, or parts of it, on flat paper. You will quickly find out how difficult this is, if you wrap a piece of paper around a globe or ball. It fits at the middle, but not at the top and bottom. Therefore, the east and west distances on the usual map may be correct at the Equator, but too great as we go north or south. Compare, for example, on a globe and a flat map, the shape and size of Greenland.

The maps on this page show how one-map-maker tried to show the world more accurately on flat paper. The other maps in this book have also been drawn to represent parts of the world quite exactly, but because of the difficulties mentioned, it is not always possible to use the scales (number of miles covered by one inch) shown for accurate measurement in every direction.

THEY WENT EXPLORING

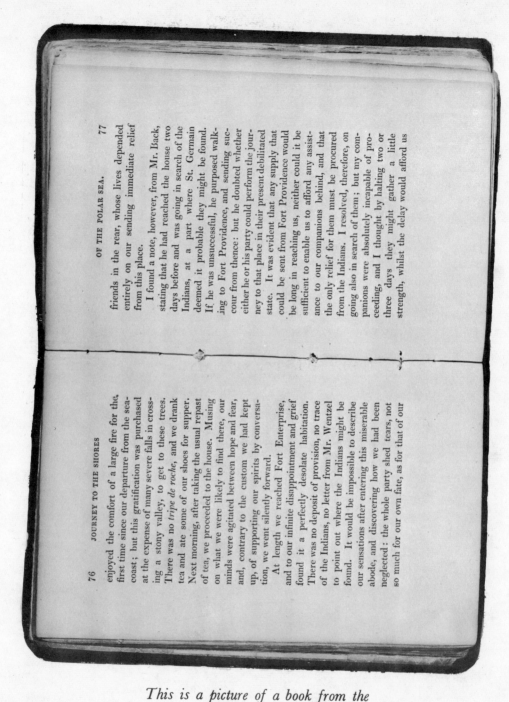

This is a picture of a book from the library of the University of Toronto,

JOURNEY TO THE SHORES OF THE POLAR SEA.

It was written by Sir John Franklin about his adventures in Northern Canada, and was published in 1829.

THEY WENT EXPLORING

Eric   Bjarni   Leif   Marco Polo   Columbus   Balboa   Diaz   da Gama   Cabot

Magellan   Drake   Tasman   Cook   Bering   Frobisher   Davis   Hudson

by R. S. LAMBERT

Illustrations by ROBERT KUNZ

A Publication of

THE BOOK SOCIETY OF CANADA LIMITED

Shackleton   Scott   Peary   Livingstone   Baker   Grant   Speke   Burton   Park

Baffin   Franklin   Bruce

Thanks are due to C. S. Hammond & Company for permission to use the basic maps for the end-papers.

Printed in Canada

PEOPLE IN THIS BOOK

INSIDE AFRICA—HOW IT WAS EXPLORED

DARING FEATS OF EXPLORATION

ABOUT THIS BOOK

IT HAS taken us thousands of years to explore the surface of the world. The earliest explorers had to travel without knowing where they were going, or what dangers and hardships they would encounter. They had little written information and few instruments or machines to assist them.

Until about one hundred years ago, boats were propelled by human muscle or by the wind. How helpless men must have felt in such craft, buffeted by stormy seas, and driven by ocean currents and contrary winds. Until the compass was invented, sailors had to steer by the sun and stars, and often there would be long periods when they could see neither.

Until about fifty years ago, men had to journey on foot into unknown places, often carrying their food and baggage on their backs or dragging it on sleighs or toboggans. Sometimes they used dogs, horses or other animals to help them.

Gradually explorers became better equipped. Each learned from those who had gone before. The invention of the compass, the quadrant, the chronometer and other instruments gave explorers a feeling of assurance that they did not have before; with them they were able to calculate just where they were.

Then, in 1833, the first ship crossed the ocean under steam-power. Man now had a boat that could go where he directed it, in spite of winds and currents, and could pass through ice fields that were passable at all.

The invention of the steam engine was followed by that of the gasoline engine, and in 1903 man succeeded in flying. In later years he so greatly improved the aeroplane that it could be used in exploring unknown parts of the earth, very difficult to reach in any other way. Think what the ability to get up off the ground, above the trees and hills, meant in the work of exploration! We can hardly realize that a journey across the sea that used to take four weeks one hundred years ago, can now be made in less than twenty-four hours. A land journey of three hundred miles into the wilderness that took three weeks only about fifty years ago, can now be made by air in two hours.

However, the last great discovery, the conquest of Mount Everest, was made by men on foot, although without the help of a recent invention, the bottling of oxygen, their climb to over 29,000 feet above sea level, would not have been possible.

In this book you will read about brave men who travelled to far-off places, and made the wide world known to all of us. You may imagine yourself the leader of a band of men adventuring in the Arctic, in darkest Africa or the wide Pacific.

By travelling with the explorers in this book and by studying the illustrations, you will gain useful knowledge of the geography of the world, and will find out why these men undertook their perilous journeys. Each had one or more of the following reasons: desire to gain wealth for himself; wish to add to his country's wealth, territory and glory; readiness to endure great hardships because he was employed to do so.

Some had a great desire to help the poor and sick, others to bring the story of Christianity to native peoples. Last of all, the love of adventure and of doing things no one else had done before, drove others forward to face danger in strange places.

How many qualities of a great explorer have you?

Baker Livingstone Peary Scott Shackleton Byrd Hillary Tensing

SEEKING NEW HOMES IN THE WEST

THE NORSEMEN IN AMERICA

A THOUSAND years ago, when there were no television sets, no radios, and no printed books, people knew very little about the world they lived in.

They thought the world was flat like a plate, with the land lying in the middle like a piece of meat, and the sea flowing around it like gravy. Anything that might be spilled over the edge would fall down into a dark hole underneath! They were afraid to venture far out of sight of land, to "see the world", for fear of not getting back home again.

There were some people, however, who travelled great distances. Since there were no roads, they went by sea, in boats. The bravest of these were the Norsemen (the word "norse" means *north*). They lived in north-western Europe. Their descendants, the peoples of Norway, Denmark, and Sweden, live there still.

This part of Europe is shaped like a big horse's head with its mouth open, and juts out far into the sea. Above the coast mountains tower, covered with thin

9

Fiords are long arms of the sea, usually with steep sides. Perhaps they were dug out by glaciers, thousands of years ago. They make excellent shelter for small boats.

soil. On the lower slopes of the mountains grow fine evergreen trees. Between the mountains are narrow, rocky valleys up which the sea flows. These long arms of the sea are called fiords. The Norsemen probably did not cross the mountains, or know much about the land that lay back of them

They lived along the coast, and made the best use of what they had. In this northern land the winters were long and cold, and the summers short. It was not a good country for raising crops, such as wheat. The Norsemen cut down trees and built ships from the wood. In these ships they fished, first in the fiords, then in the shallow waters off the coast. They found that the winds blew a stream of warm water from the south along their shores. This stream of warm water kept the sea from freezing, even in the coldest weather. The Norsemen could fish all year round.

They were good sailors, because they were not afraid of the sea. They worshipped *Woden*, the god of the sky, *Thor*, the god of thunder, and *Tiu*, the god of war. They thought the best way of pleasing their gods was to live a brave, wild life, and at the end to die fighting in battle.

In the rock of the mountains the Norsemen found iron, which they dug out and hammered into spears, swords, and axes for war. They also made nails from the iron, and used them to build bigger and better ships, in which they could travel longer distances.

Some of the Norsemen's ships were built for fighting. These were long and narrow, with one mast, a large sail, and many oars. They would hold many fighters, with their weapons and horses.

Others of their ships were built for trading. These were short, broad, and had sails but no oars. Inside

Without power drills and explosives, mining iron in the early days was tedious work. It is thought that, with the cooling of the earth, certain gases became solids — one of these was iron ore.

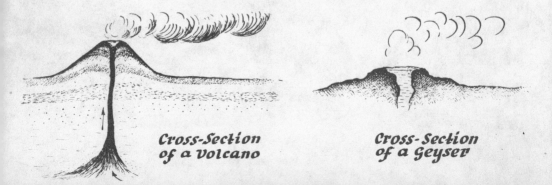

Cross-Section of a Volcano

Cross-Section of a Geyser

there was room to carry food, cattle, and trading goods, such as fish, iron, and ivory, which the Norsemen got from walrus tusks.

In their ships the Norsemen used to go "a-viking" (that is, a-wandering) from place to place. Sometimes they were called Vikings. They sailed along the coasts of Europe, and landed in England, France, Germany, and other countries. When they landed, sometimes they traded goods. More often, they attacked and plundered the villages they found. The people of Europe became afraid of them. "The Vikings are coming! God save us from their fury!" was a cry that would send everyone into hiding.

There came a time when there were so many Norsemen there was not enough food for them in their own country. Then they began to look for other lands to live in. Often the sea washed up, on their shores, bits of wood, strange plants, and other things which seemed to have come from the West, a long way off. This made the Norsemen think there must be other lands beyond the sea. They decided to find out.

Some of the Norsemen put to sea and sailed west. After travelling about 600 miles, they reached an island with low shores, on which it was easy to build houses. In the middle of the island, however, were mountains, with fire and smoke blowing out of their tops. These burning mountains were volcanoes.

This new land was as far north as their homeland, and had quite as cold a climate. The Norsemen called it Iceland. It was not a "land of ice", of course. In some parts of Iceland springs of hot water spurted from the earth, warming the soil, and making the grass grow well. Cattle could be pastured here, and crops grown. In the sea around Iceland were seals, whales, and fish.

A Hot Spring

A Volcano

There must be very great heat in the centre of the earth, because here and there, all over the world, hot water and hot, melted rock (lava) come to the surface. The lava is thrown from the interior of the earth through the craters of the volcanoes. It solidifies where it falls. The hot water is from the surface. It has sunk down into the earth and become heated. Then it rises to the surface as hot springs or geysers. In a geyser the water is discharged high into the air at intervals, as steam pressure is built up.

Eric the Red

Among the Norsemen who came to Iceland and settled was Eric the Red, so-called because he had a long, red beard. Eric had killed a man, and been forced to leave the homeland. In Iceland, he fell into more trouble, and had to leave that country. Where was he to go?

Eric put out to sea and sailed farther westward, looking for a new home. When he had gone about 200 miles, he sighted a land of rocks and snow-covered mountains. Between the mountains ran rivers of ice, called glaciers. There were no trees, and it did not look as if anything could grow there.

He sailed along the shore of this land, and near its southern end found places where it curved into bays. These made good harbours for ships, because they were protected from the winds. There were streams of fresh water flowing into the bays, patches of grass, and bushes full of berries which were good to eat. Better still, there were herds of reindeer which would provide meat for his men to eat.

Eric decided to make his home here. He sailed back to Iceland, and asked his friends and relatives to join him and come out to the new land.

"What do you call the place?" they asked him.

"Greenland," answered Eric. He was afraid that, if his friends knew it was a land of ice and snow, they would not come. So he pretended it was a land of green grass and good pasture. About 500 people went to Greenland with Eric, in twenty-five ships.

When they reached their new home they saw it was not green at all. But there was enough grass for their cattle, game to hunt, and the streams were full of salmon. They were glad to stay, and went on calling this great island Greenland. That is still its name today.

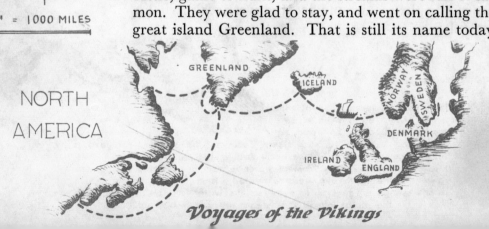

N

1" = 1000 MILES

NORTH AMERICA

GREENLAND

ICELAND

NORWAY

SWEDEN

DENMARK

IRELAND

ENGLAND

Voyages of the Vikings

Bjarni

If you were a giant, and wanted to go from Europe to the continent of North America in three steps, you would first step on Iceland, then on Greenland, and lastly, on America, Today, aeroplanes flying to our country often follow this route.

In their search for new lands the Norsemen had "stepped" from Europe to Iceland, and then to Greenland. The third step would take them—where?

Soon after Eric the Red and his friends had settled in Greenland, another man, called Bjarni, left his home in Iceland to join them.

For many days Bjarni's ship was driven west by a gale. Then it drifted through thick fog. Bjarni had no idea how far he had come, or where he was. Nowadays sailors can steer their ships by a compass, the needle of which always points to the north. Bjarni had no compass. He could only tell where he was by looking at the sun and the stars. These could only be seen in good weather.

When the fog cleared, Bjarni found himself in sight of a land of low hills and many trees, and Bjarni did not think it could be Greenland. Supposing he must have been blown too far south, he steered his ship north-east, and came to a flat land with many trees. He thought that this could not be Greenland, either.

He sailed on before a south-west wind, and sighted land a third time! This land was mountainous, and covered with snow and glaciers. His crew was tired of the sea, and wanted to land there, but Bjarni said, "It is only an island, and good for nothing."

He sailed on and, in four days' time, reached the south-east tip of Greenland.

Bjarni, as you have guessed, had reached North America, but he had not even bothered to land there!

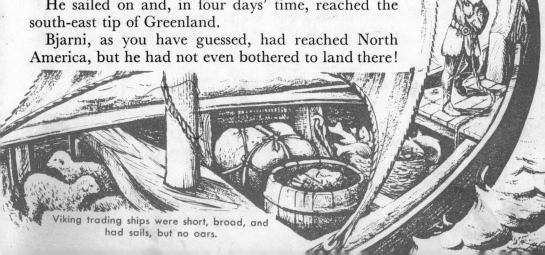

Viking trading ships were short, broad, and had sails, but no oars.

Leif the Lucky

Eric the Red had a son. He was called Leif Erickson. This means "Leif, the son of Eric". Wishing his son to be educated, Eric sent Leif to Norway, to serve at the court of the King of Norway, Olaf.

Before Leif arrived there, King Olaf and his people had become Christians. They had stopped worshipping Woden, Thor, and Tiu, and had faith in the one, true God. Leif, too, became a Christian, and when it was time for him to return home to Greenland, King Olaf said to him, "Leif, tell your people in Greenland what you have learned here. Ask Eric and all his people to become Christians like us."

Leif sailed home, and did his best. He persuaded nearly all the Greenlanders to become Christians, except Eric. His father would not give up his gods.

In his father's house Leif met Bjarni, and heard his story about finding a new land. Leif thought he would explore this land. Perhaps it would be good to live in. What if he could persuade the people there to become Christians!

Salmon

Leif bought Bjarni's ship, and took a crew of thirty-five men with him. He sailed in the year 1000, and followed the same course as Bjarni. However Leif went the other way around. That is, he visited *first*, the place that Bjarni had found *last*.

First Leif came to the land of rocks and glaciers. Although he landed there, he saw it would not be a good place for settlement, because there was no grass for the cattle. Leif had reached Labrador, on the north-east coast of Canada.

Next he came to a low, sandy shore, behind which great forests grew. He landed again, and named the country "Mark-Land", or "Land of Woods". This

The Norsemen decided to winter here .

was probably the south-west tip of Nova Scotia.

Sailing on before a north-east wind, Leif came to an island, lying close to the mainland. Here a river emptied into the sea. Leif and his men landed close to the river and built huts. They found big salmon in the river, and plenty of grass on the river banks for the cattle to eat. The Norsemen decided to winter there.

Leif's men explored inland, and found wild grapes growing. They cut bunches of these and took them back to the ship. They cut down trees, and filled their ship with a good cargo of timber.

They were surprised to find that the winter was mild, with almost no frost. The winter days were not as short as they were in Greenland. This was because they were farther south.

When spring came, Leif decided to sail home and make a report on the new land. "I will give it a name," he said. "I call it Vineland the Good, after the grapes we have gathered and eaten here."

It is thought that Vineland was the country just south of Chesapeake Bay, on the east coast of what is now the United States.

Leif Erickson did not make another voyage to the New World, but his brother and many other Norsemen sailed west from Greenland to try to find the land where Leif had spent the winter. Some of them explored the coast of Canada, and others sailed as far south as the Hudson River. They were probably the first white men to set foot where the city of New York now stands. Wild wheat, as well as grapes, grew there, and they thought it might be Vineland.

Before long they met red-skinned men with broad cheeks, large eyes, and long, matted hair. These men came in canoes. At first they were friendly and traded

SUNDAY

MONDAY

TUESDAY
from Tiu

WEDNESDAY
from Woden

THURSDAY
from Thor

FRIDAY
from Frig,
wife of Woden

SATURDAY

Some of the days of the week are named after the Norse gods.

What places in this bird's-eye map can you recognize?

furs with the Norsemen, getting cloth and milk in return. Then one day a bull, belonging to the Norsemen, frightened them by bellowing and charging. The red-skins became angry, and attacked the Norsemen with bows and arrows, killing some of them. The white men decided this was not a good place to settle, and sailed back to Greenland.

Others who come out to look for Vineland were also driven off by the Indians. Then the Norsemen began to think that it cost a great deal to build ships and furnish them with goods for an expedition to the New World. Their country, Greenland, was so poor that they could not really afford these voyages.

At last they gave up the search for the wonderful land which Leif had described, and said he should be called "Leif the Lucky", because he was the only one who had been able to find Vineland the Good.

Poets and minstrels kept many stories of long ago from being forgotten until they were printed in books.

Later ships stopped sailing from Iceland to Greenland. There was nothing there to trade. In the end, the Norsemen in Greenland died out.

Sometimes the Icelanders had feasts, and at these poets told stories of the brave deeds and long voyages of the Vikings. They told the adventures of Eric the Red, of Bjarni, and of Leif the Lucky. Because of this, their deeds were not forgotten.

If people had known how to print and make books in those days, these stories would have been read by other people all over Europe. But there were no printed books for nearly 500 years after the time of Leif.

However the Norsemen travelled all over Europe, going a-viking and trading. It is quite likely that sailors as far away as England, Spain, and Italy heard some of these tales about Leif and the New World.

Do you think they would want to look for Vineland too?

EARLY TRADERS
GO EAST

MARCO POLO

LONG ago there lived in Venice, a city in Italy, a boy named Marco Polo. Venice was built on islands. It had no streets or sidewalks. Between the rows of houses were waterways, called canals. People travelled along these canals in long, narrow boats, called gondolas, pushed by long poles. Venice was beautiful and gay, and Marco lived happily there.

There was always something exciting happening in Venice, because it was a city built right on the sea. The Venetians, as the people of Venice were called, had hardly any soil to till near their houses, so they could not grow their own food. Instead, they lived by trading with other countries. Their trade was carried on in ships that sailed to and fro between Venice and the countries of the East.

Marco loved watching these ships come and go. Many of the things he liked best came from the East. There was the silk of which his best clothes were made, the gold pieces (money) men jingled in their pockets, and the spices that his mother put into his food so it would be tasty. Marco's mother used a great deal of cinnamon, nutmeg, ginger, cloves, and pepper in

17

her cooking. She had no refrigerator, and her food would have quickly spoiled if she had not put spices in it. But all these spices cost a great deal of money, because they had to be brought such a long way.

To get these things, Marco knew that the Venetian traders had to go on long, dangerous journeys. They had to travel over land as well as by sea. At sea, they had to avoid pirates. On land, they had to escape robbers and wild beasts. When they reached the cities of the East, they had to do business with the Arabs, who always tried to get the better of them.

In starting a voyage, the Venetian traders loaded their ships with cargoes of salt, fish, wool, and iron. These things were brought to Venice overland from the west of Europe. Then they would set out with a favourable wind, and put into port at Alexandria, in Egypt, or some other great eastern city.

Here they would sell their goods to the Arabs. The Arabs would not pay for them in money, but gave the Venetians silk, gold, and spices in exchange.

The Arabs said they had brought their goods on the backs of camels, from lands still farther off in the East. Some of the things came from India, some from Japan, China, and the islands of the South Seas.

The Venetians had never seen these lands themselves. They were glad they had no need to go there, but could trade with the Arabs in cities that were closer to Venice. They took home the silk, gold, and spices they had bought. Some of these goods they used. Some, they sold right in Venice. The rest were sold at a high price to the peoples of Western Europe.

Nicolo Polo, Marco's father, was a trader. In the year Marco was born, his father and his uncle, Maffeo Polo, set out on a trading trip to the East.

In Marco's day there were no railroads, and goods were carried overland on the backs of animals to seaports, from which they were carried farther by ships. Venice was such a seaport.

VENICE

ALEXANDRIA

At home in Venice, Marco's mother waited—one year—two years—three years—. In those days there was no radio, no way of sending a telegram, or even a letter. Marco's mother died without knowing what had happened to her husband.

When fifteen years had passed, people said the Polos must have been shipwrecked, or have died of cold or hunger, or have been robbed and murdered by the Turks, who were enemies of the people of Venice. But none of this was true, because, in that very year, Nicolo and Maffeo came home. They had a wonderful story to tell Marco and their friends.

They said they had been among the Mongols, a people who lived far away in the East, in the middle of Asia. There, it was very hot in summer, and bitterly cold in winter. The land was flat, and without trees. It grew short grass, but no crops. The Mongols had no settled homes. They wandered about in bands—men, women, children, horses, and cattle. They lived in tents, and ate meat and drank milk. They spent much of their time riding on horseback, and were very warlike and cruel.

Some time before Marco was born, these Mongols found they had not enough grassland to feed their horses and cattle. Then they moved into the lands of their neighbours, who lived in houses in cities, or on farms, just as we do today. The Mongols killed nearly everyone who stood in their way.

At that time the Mongols had a great leader, called Genghis Khan. He first made war on the Turks, who lived in the west of Asia, and defeated them. Then he conquered another country, Cathay (or China) in the Far East. By this time he ruled over nearly all Asia.

1" = 400 MILES

BAGHDAD

The Arabs brought their goods on the backs of camels from lands farther east.

Still Genghis Khan was not satisfied. He thought he would next attack Europe. Perhaps he might even have captured Venice, but suddenly he died, and quarrels broke out among his sons. All the land Genghis had ruled was divided among them. When Marco was born, the largest part (including Cathay) was ruled by his grandson, Kublai Khan.

Nicolo and Maffeo Polo said they had visited Kublai Khan in Cathay, and lived in his palace for two years. He had treated them as friends, and asked them many questions about the way people lived in Venice.

The Polos were just as interested in Cathay, because they hoped to open up trade there. They also hoped that Kublai Khan and his Mongols would become Christians.

Kublai did not promise to do this. However, he asked the Polos to bring him some teachers to instruct his people, and some holy oil from Jerusalem, when they came again to Cathay.

Then he gave them a golden tablet, like a large medal, and they returned home to Venice.

As he told these stories, Nicolo Polo saw that Marco was listening eagerly. One day he said, "Marco, you have grown up to be a strong, clever lad. Would you like to come with us on our next journey to Cathay?"

You may be sure Marco lost no time in saying yes. Here was his chance to see the world!

In 1271 (nearly 700 years ago) the Polos set out on their second trip to Cathay, and this time Marco went with them. They were not able to take the teachers for whom Kublai had asked, because none of them was willing to face so long a journey.

The Polos set sail from Venice in a long, narrow ship, with one mast and a broad sail, and many oars

for use when there was no wind. They took food and bedding with them.

They sailed the length of the Adriatic Sea, and across the Mediterranean Sea to the coast of Palestine. The voyage took them a whole month! Then they made an overland journey to Jerusalem to get the holy oil for Kublai Khan.

They returned to Acre, on the coast of Palestine, where they joined a caravan, or group of traders, travelling together for safety. They had an Arab to guide them.

It was a long way from the coast of Palestine to Cathay, even if the Polos could have gone direct, for there were no trains, busses, or even roads to travel on. They had to go on foot, or ride on mules, or camels, one behind the other.

Before they started overland, Nicolo took out his golden tablet that Kublai had given him. "This is our safe conduct," he explained to Marco. "It commands all the great Khan's servants to help us wherever we go. On it our lives depend."

The first part of their journey took them near Mount Ararat, where Noah's Ark came to rest when the Flood was over. Then they turned south, making their way through mountain valleys. At one place Marco saw a "fountain of oil" flowing from the ground. People came from far off to get this oil to burn in their lamps.

Then they followed a broad river, on whose shores grew date palms and olive trees. At last they came to the city of Baghdad, which you may have read about in the story of *Ali Baba and the Forty Thieves*. Here they saw Arab traders who had rolls of silk, embroidered with gold thread, and carpets with

Descendants of the rug weavers Marco saw, today weave some of the most beautiful and long-wearing rugs produced anywhere in the world.

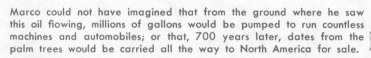

Marco could not have imagined that from the ground where he saw this oil flowing, millions of gallons would be pumped to run countless machines and automobiles; or that, 700 years later, dates from the palm trees would be carried all the way to North America for sale.

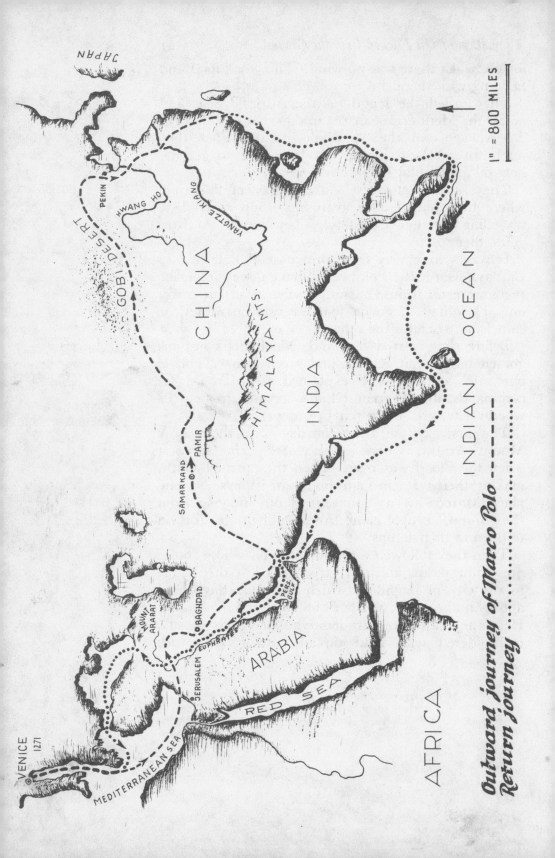

JAPAN

PEKIN

HWANG HO

YANGTZE KIANG

GOBI DESERT

CHINA

HIMALAYA MTS.

INDIA

SAMARKAND

PAMIR

INDIAN OCEAN

MOUNT ARARAT

BAGHDAD

EUPHRATES

PERSIAN GULF

JERUSALEM

ARABIA

RED SEA

AFRICA

VENICE
1271

MEDITERRANEAN SEA

1" = 800 MILES

Outward journey of Marco Polo - - - - -
Return journey · · · · · · · · ·

patterns of birds and beasts. Marco watched his father and uncle as they traded. Soon he was a good trader himself.

Now they left Baghdad, still following the river, and travelled south through the land where Abraham was born, which you read about in the Old Testament. It took them many months to reach the Persian Gulf. Today we can travel from Baghdad to the sea in a day or two, by automobile.

Because there were great mountains between them and Cathay, they could not go the shortest way. These mountains were too high to climb. They had to find a way through, by following the valleys that lay between them. In some places there were deserts to cross. These were open, sandy spaces, where little rain fell, and no grass or crops grew. Sometimes the wind would blow up into sandstorms, and then travellers would lose their way.

The Polos did not travel every day. Marco had time for sport, as well as work. His chief sport was hunting game. Sometimes he shot this game with bow and arrows. Sometimes trained hawks were used in hunting smaller birds, and animals.

When they reached the sea, the Polos planned to go the rest of the way to Cathay by ship. But they saw that the boats were small and not safe, so they turned inland again. They travelled northward, then eastward, through mountain passes. Once they visited a place in the mountains where rubies were dug out of mines.

Then they came to a highland, as flat as a table top, which their guide told them was "the roof of

Rubies are found in limestone rocks. In Marco's day these stones were called *carbuncles*, which means "burning coals".

In mountainous country in Marco's time, as in ours, roads and trails followed the valleys and passes between the mountains to avoid unnecessary hard climbing. Watch for this when you are travelling through hilly country.

the world". It was so cold that no birds flew. However they saw flocks of big mountain sheep with long horns and thick wool. This kind of sheep still live there, and are called "Polo's sheep", after Marco Polo.

When they came down from the highland, or plateau, they entered the great Gobi Desert of China. Here each day's journey was measured by the distance from one water spring to the next. Everyone suffered from dust, lack of food, and thirst. In the noonday heat they often saw pools of water in the distance. Imagine their disappointment when they hastened forward only to find that there was no pool there! It was only a mirage! Desert travellers are still fooled by such mirages.

Three and a half years had now passed since the Polos had left Venice, when one day Marco saw a great cloud of dust on the horizon.

"Is that another sandstorm?" he asked his uncle.

"No," said Maffeo Polo. "Those are messengers from the Great Khan who are sent to welcome us."

Presently the cloud turned into a troop of fierce Mongol horsemen, with narrow, slant eyes, who told the Polos they had come to take them to the palace.

On the fortieth day after this, the Polos came into a great park with a high wall around it, and in the middle a marble palace. In the palace they found the Great Khan. They bowed before him to the ground, and presented him with the holy oil.

After a time Kublai noticed Marco standing behind his father.

"Who is that young man?" he asked.

"Sire," replied Nicolo, "he is my son, the dearest thing to me in the whole world. I have brought him to serve you."

The Polos found wild sheep on the Pamir Plateau, where it was cold, and there was little rainfall (because the rain-bearing winds had lost their moisture before reaching this height). Only grass would grow in this climate and soil.

The great Gobi Desert is ¾ of the total area of China. It is desert land because it lies hundreds of miles from any sea coast. The winds, whether blowing from the east or west, have lost their moisture by the time they reach it, and bring no rain.

The Khan liked Marco, and invited him to live in the palace, where he showed him his treasures. Here Marco saw "paper money" being made from the bark of mulberry trees, which grow in most parts of China. The Chinese were the first people to make paper money (like our dollar bills), and to print words on paper.

Kublai also showed Marco how his palace was heated with "black stones", or coal, which was not used for fuel in Europe at that time.

Kublai made Marco one of his messengers, and sent him all over his kingdom to carry orders and make reports. In this way, Marco learned a great deal about China.

He learned that, in North China the summers were short, and the farmers could harvest only one crop each year. The land was dry, except where the great river Hwang-Ho flooded its banks.

But in South China it was hot, and there was plenty of rain. The farmers there grew rice, and could harvest two, or even three crops in one year. They planted the rice (which looks like long grass) on low land covered with water.

The main food of millions of Chinese is still rice.

Where the mulberry trees grew, the farmers picked the leaves, and fed them to silk-worms. These worms made cocoons by spinning silk threads out of their bodies, as a spider spins thread for its web. In the cities men carefully unwound these threads and made silk cloth from them.

Even today, silk is made in the same way.

On his travels Marco learned about other countries near to China, such as India, Malaya, and Japan. He also heard of a land to the north, where there

Silk worm

cocoon

silk cover

chrysalis

eggs

moths

Real silk is made by the silkworm, which feeds on mulberry leaves.

Rice plants are grown from seed, until they are about 8" high. They are then set out in rows by hand in fields or paddies, which are covered by a few inches of water. This water is put on the land by a simple water wheel, or by an irrigation dike. When the rice begins to head the soil is allowed to dry.

were white bears and dogs, which were used to drag sleds over the ice and snow. What land do you think this was?

The Polos had hoped Kublai Khan would become a Christian, but he did not do so. After living many years in Cathay, the Polos returned home to Venice, travelling most of the way by ship this time.

At first no one in Venice could recognize them, because they had been away over twenty-five years and were much changed. But, when they ripped open the seams of their clothing, rubies, sapphires, pearls, and diamonds fell out. Then everyone agreed they could be none other than the Polos, and welcomed them home.

Marco had been a young man when he left Venice. Now he was a man as old as your own father. When he told people about his adventures many of them would not believe him. Others said he was telling the truth.

"But, in that case," they added, "the world must be much larger than we thought!"

Because of Marco's story, many traders wanted to go to the Far East, but they were afraid, because they had no golden tablet from the Great Khan to protect them on the overland journey.

They began to look for a new way of getting to Cathay that would be shorter and less dangerous.

Marco wrote a book about his adventures which many people read. It made them even more anxious to learn what the world was like.

Some day you may read *The Travels of Marco Polo*, the story of one of the longest journeys ever recorded in the history of man.

Did you ever see a bamboo fish pole? It was made from the stalk of the bamboo plant.

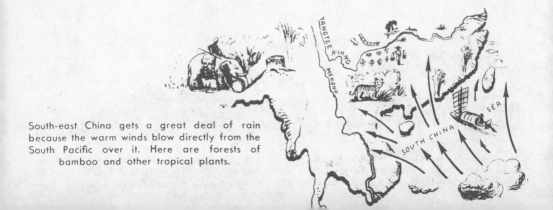

South-east China gets a great deal of rain because the warm winds blow directly from the South Pacific over it. Here are forests of bamboo and other tropical plants.

SEEKING TRADE IN
INDIA AND THE ISLES

COLUMBUS

MANY years after the time of Marco Polo, there lived in Genoa, a city not far from Venice, a cloth-weaver named Columbus. He had a son, Christopher, whom he was training to be a weaver like himself.

But one day the boy said, "Father, I would like to go to sea."

"To sea, Christopher," exclaimed his father. "Well, if you work hard at your weaving, I will let you go out sometimes with our fishing fleet."

Columbus liked going with these boats, because some of them went trading as well as fishing. The seamen of Genoa often made trips to the eastern end of the Mediterranean Sea. Here, like the Venetians, they traded with the Arabs and brought silks, gold, and spices back to Genoa.

His father soon saw that Christopher would never settle down to be a weaver, and allowed him to go on trading trips whenever he had the chance. Before long Christopher became a skilled navigator. He learned how to draw maps and make charts. Also he knew how to use a compass to find out in which direction a ship was sailing.

27

Genoa was almost as important a seaport as Venice. Behind it were safe passes through the mountains, so that wheat and other goods could be brought down from the plain to the north. These goods were loaded on ships, taken to the East, and traded for spices, etc.

The Arabs are supposed to have invented the compass. The first of these were very simple — a magnet afloat on a bowl of water.

1" = 568 MILES

ATLANTIC

OCEAN

Soon Christopher noticed that the Genoese (men of Genoa) were not doing well with their trading. He asked why this was, and was told it was because the Turks had spread into Eastern Europe. They were followers of the prophet Mohammed, and attacked Christian ships to prevent them from trading with the Arabs. The Turks wanted to control this rich Eastern trade themselves.

Columbus took part in many sea-fights between the Genoese and the Turks. Often the Genoese were beaten, and had to return home without exchanging their cargoes for Eastern goods. Trade was so bad that many of the people of Genoa became poor.

Sometimes Christopher heard people say, "If only there were someone like Marco Polo, who could go across Asia and find the great Khan of Cathay! Perhaps he could persuade him to turn Christian. Then the Khan might attack the heathen Turks from the East, while we were attacking them from the West. Between us, we might be able to defeat the Turks!"

Christopher knew that no one could travel across Asia to China now, as Marco Polo had done. The Turks blocked the way. However he thought he might be able to do better than Polo.

By this time scientists knew something that Marco Polo had not known. They knew that the world was round. Christopher thought that perhaps he could reach Cathay by going not east, but west.

West of Genoa, the Atlantic Ocean and the Mediterranean Sea are joined by a narrow passage of water known as the Straits of Gibraltar. Columbus planned to sail past Gibraltar and visit some of the countries on the shores of the Atlantic.

He was now in charge of a ship, and made trading voyages to Portugal, England, and perhaps Iceland.

Columbus engaged in sea-fights with the Turks.

Possibly he heard in Iceland the tale of Leif the Lucky and the discovery of Vineland. Certainly he must have heard stories about bits of timber and strange plants being washed up on the west coast of Europe. Where had these come from? Perhaps they had drifted right across the Atlantic from Cathay!

One day Columbus's ship was wrecked on the coast of Portugal. He landed safely, and made his way to Lisbon, the capital city. He liked Lisbon so much that he settled there and married a Portuguese woman. He lived by selling maps which he drew or copied.

Lisbon has a good harbour at the mouth of a river which flows into the Atlantic Ocean. The Portuguese were good seamen, and had been encouraged to go exploring by the King's son, Prince Henry.

Prince Henry was interested in the new ideas of the scientists about the shape of the earth. He had studied the sun, moon, stars, and ocean tides. Although he never went exploring himself, he gave money and ships to seamen to search for new countries with which Portugal might trade. For this reason people called him "Prince Henry the Navigator."

Some of the seamen he sent out discovered islands lying to the south-west of Portugal. Among these were the Madeira, the Azores, and the Cape Verde Islands. Columbus thought the Azores might be halfway to Cathay.

Other seamen sailed southward from Portugal to explore the west coast of Africa. They found gold, ivory (from elephants' tusks), and pepper there. The climate was very hot, and made white men ill.

The natives of Africa were black, and the Portuguese took some of them home to Lisbon to be their servants. They found they could get more money by bringing

AZORES ISLANDS

MADEIRA ISLANDS
CANARY ISLANDS

Prince Henry sent expeditions to islands off the coast of Africa, and to Africa itself.

PORTUGAL

AFRICA

N

1" = 1760 MILES

EQUATOR

black men home and selling them, than by trading in ivory and gold. So they traded in black slaves.

Columbus sailed on a trading voyage to Africa. But all the time he was thinking: How can I get a ship to try sailing west across the Atlantic, to find Cathay!

Although Columbus knew the world was round, he did not know how large it was. He thought the distance across the Atlantic Ocean from Europe to Asia (where Cathay was) could easily be sailed. He had no idea that any big land lay between them.

By this time, Prince Henry the Navigator, who might have helped him, was dead. So Columbus asked his brother, John, now King of Portugal, to supply a ship for his voyages. But John refused. He said all his ships were busy trading, or exploring in West Africa.

Soon afterwards Columbus left Lisbon and moved into Spain, the country east of Portugal. He visited King Ferdinand and Queen Isabella of Spain, and laid his plans before them. He showed them a map of the world which he had drawn.

Queen Isabella liked Columbus. She persuaded King Ferdinand to appoint a committee of scientists to look over the plans for the voyage. At the end of five years this committee gave its report.

"It will take Columbus three years," its members said, "to reach Asia by sailing west, and no one knows what dangers lie in his way. Even if he arrives there, he will find himself on the other side of the globe with no means of getting back home."

It took Columbus two more years to answer these men, and persuade the King and Queen to support him. At last, just as he was despairing, word came

from Queen Isabella that she would make him an admiral, and give him three ships to try his luck.

The three ships were the *Nina*, the *Pinza*, and the *Santa Maria*. The *Nina* was quite small. You could walk right along her deck from one end to the other in twenty-five paces. But she was a fast sailer, having three masts with square sails. The *Santa Maria* was the flagship, and so carried Columbus.

Columbus sailed from Palos on the 3rd of August 1492, with a crew of ninety sailors. There was so little room on the ships that the men had to sleep on bare boards on deck. Only the Admiral and his captains had cabins of their own. For food they had hard biscuit, salt meat, dried fish, and wine.

They measured time with a sand-glass before clocks and watches were invented.

Columbus steered due west across the Atlantic. He used a compass to show him what course to follow. When the weather was clear, he judged, by looking at the sun and stars, the position of his ship. He guessed its speed by watching bubbles or weeds floating past. He kept a card on which he wrote down each day the distance he thought they had travelled. He did not have a clock, but measured the time with a sand-glass.

At first the ships had steady winds behind them, and made good speed. Then the winds died away, and they were becalmed. Day after day there was no work to do on board, and the men began to grumble.

Columbus noticed great flocks of birds passing overhead, flying south-west. He remembered that the Portuguese sailors had found the Azores Islands by watching the flight of birds. He realized that these birds must be flying toward land, too. He decided to follow them, and altered his ship's course from due west to south-west.

Columbus declared he could reach India by sailing west.

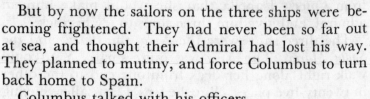

But by now the sailors on the three ships were becoming frightened. They had never been so far out at sea, and thought their Admiral had lost his way. They planned to mutiny, and force Columbus to turn back home to Spain.

Columbus talked with his officers.

"I will ask you to sail for only three more days," he told them. "Then, if no land is sighted, we will turn back."

That same night a sailor on the *Nina* picked out of the sea a branch bearing a little flower like a wild rose. Someone else scooped up a stick, a plant, and a piece of carved wood. These objects proved they must be near land.

The sailors watched eagerly all the next day and night. Just before dawn on the 12th of October, a look-out man on the *Pinza* shouted out in Spanish, "*Tierra! Tierra!*" (Land! Land!)

He had sighted a small island, lying off the east coast of North America. It was one of a group later called the Bahama Islands, where people today often go for a winter vacation.

Columbus and his captains, dressed in their best clothes and carrying gay flags, were rowed to shore in armed boats. On landing, everyone kneeled down and gave thanks to God for the safe journey. Then Columbus named the island *San Salvador* (Saint Saviour), and took possession of it in the name of Ferdinand and Isabella of Spain.

What was the island like? Columbus wrote a description of it in his *Journal*. "This Island is large and very flat, with bright green trees, much water, a large lake in the centre, without any mountain. The whole land is so green that it is a pleasure to look on it."

Now Columbus wondered where he was. He looked at the natives who had gathered on the shore to watch him. They had dark brown skins, not like the yellow skins of the Chinese. Columbus felt certain he had not yet reached the land of the Great Khan.

The natives were not Japanese, either, for the same reason. They looked more like the people of India, who also had dark skins. Perhaps, thought Columbus, I have sailed too far south for China and Japan, and have reached India, or an island off the Indian coast.

"Yes," he said, "these must be the Indies, and the people are Indians."

Although San Salvador and the other islands off the coast of America are nowhere near India, even today they are called the "West Indies", so that people will not confuse them with the "East Indies", which are the islands off the coast of India.

The Indians of San Salvador were pleased when Columbus gave them presents of beads and red caps. In return, they brought him yams (sweet potatoes), corn, cotton thread, and parrots. Trading began.

But the Spaniards were soon disappointed.

"India," they said, "is a land full of gold. Where is your gold? We want to buy some."

As soon as the natives understood what the Spaniards wanted, they showed them some small gold ornaments.

"Where did you get these?" he asked.

The Indians made signs to show that the gold had come from other islands, bigger than theirs, and not far off.

In his *Journal*, Columbus wrote: "I intend to go on and see if I can find the Island of Japan."

Then began an exciting search for larger islands and more gold. Columbus visited Cuba, where he saw cacao beans growing, out of which cocoa and

Products of the New World

Columbus's first Voyage

AZORES IS.

LISBON
PALOS

1493

MADEIRA IS.

CANARY IS.

1492

SAN SALVADOR

CUBA

HAITI

ATLANTIC
OCEAN

N

1" = 1100 MILES

chocolate are made. He also saw natives smoking the leaves of a plant. This was tobacco. Then he sailed on to Haiti, where at last he found a few gold mines, worked by the Indians.

Although these islands did not have as much gold as Columbus had expected, he liked their pleasant climate. He saw that the soil was good for growing crops, and thought that white men could live there.

On Christmas Eve 1492, Columbus was asleep in his cabin on board the *Santa Maria*, when the ship struck a coral reef and was wrecked. Only a few lives were lost, but Columbus had now too many men to take home to Spain in the two ships that remained.

So he left part of his crew behind on Haiti, where they built a fort out of the timbers of the wrecked ship. Columbus promised these men to return later, and then set sail for Spain, in January 1493.

On his arrival he hurried to Barcelona, the city where King Ferdinand and Queen Isabella were staying.

Columbus explained that although he had not yet found Cathay, or Japan, he had found "The Indies". Then he brought out nuggets of gold, and introduced six native chiefs dressed in fine robes and carrying parrots. All these he had brought back on board his ships. Also, he showed them some cacao beans, wild cotton, and other plants he had found in the "Indies". Lastly, he showed his maps and charts and the *Journal* he had kept of his voyage.

The King and Queen were delighted with Columbus's story. They richly rewarded him, and gave him the title "Admiral of the Ocean Sea, Viceroy and Governor of the Indies". Then they asked him to take another, larger fleet of ships across the Atlantic, and explore farther.

Products of the New World

These were his instructions: "You are to look more carefully for gold, since the supply of gold in Europe is very low. You are to choose a place with a good harbour, fertile soil, and a healthful climate for white people. Here we shall send Spaniards to settle. In time a great city may be built, which will be the centre of trade in the Indies. You are appointed the first Governor of the new settlement, and shall have a share of the profits of all trade between the Indies and Spain."

The rest of the story of Columbus is rather sad. His second expedition was a failure. The fort on Haiti had been destroyed by the Indians. The new settlement he founded did not do well. The climate in summer was too hot for the Spaniards. They refused to work, and began quarrelling among themselves.

Columbus ordered the Indians to bring him gold, But, in fact, there was very little gold to be found anywhere in the West Indies. When the natives failed to bring enough of this precious metal to satisfy him, Columbus forced them to work for him and his men.

The Indians were not strong people. They were not accustomed to work hard. They lost heart, grew sick, and died.

Columbus explored many new islands, including Jamaica and Trinidad. Since no gold came from these places, King Ferdinand and Queen Isabella soon grew tired of him. They sent out another governor to rule over his settlement, and called him home to Spain.

There he died, a disappointed man.

Columbus had led the way to North America, but he himself never landed on the North American mainland. He did not even know for sure that it existed. He thought there was only a large group of islands

Mosquito

Eggs

Larva

Pupa

Adult

The Spaniards called this insect *mosquito*, which, in their language means "little fly".

Mosquitoes gave the Spaniards malarial fever.

NORTH
AMERICA

N

EQUATOR

SOUTH
AMERICA

N

with a sea-passage somewhere, leading through to Asia.

Those who came after him did much better. They spent less time looking for gold, and were content to settle down and make their homes in the New World. They found that the warm climate was good, not only for growing the native plants, such as corn and pumpkins, but also many other plants that grew elsewhere. For instance, orange trees were brought over from Spain to the West Indies, and did well there.

Later on, they discovered the mainland of America. There, in Central and South America, the Spaniards found the gold, silver, and other precious metals that they wanted so badly. They brought this gold and silver back to Spain, and so made her for a short time the richest country in Europe.

Today there are no Spanish possessions left in America, not even in the West Indies. But there are still many traces of Spain to be seen all over America. In Mexico, and in many of the countries of Central and South America, all the people speak Spanish.

The name "America" is not Spanish. It is taken from the name of an Italian seaman, named Amerigo Vespucci, who sailed on a later voyage with some of Columbus's men. He borrowed the charts and records that the old Admiral had made, and used them in a book which he wrote. In this book he pretended he had explored the New World himself.

People were so deceived by this book that they started calling the new continent "Amerigo's Land", or, for short, "America".

Gold and Silver

There was gold and silver in the New World, but Columbus did not find it.

Balboa

Columbus's idea that there was a sea-passage through the West Indies, leading to Asia, was soon found to be a mistake.

In 1513 Balboa, a Spanish captain, landed on the mainland of America at Panama, to search for the passage. He and his little band tramped through tropical jungles, where some of the men fell sick with *malaria*, a fever carried by mosquitoes.

At last Balboa led the way over a mountain, from the top of which they could see, to the West, another ocean, blue and shining in the sun.

Balboa saw that he had found, not a sea-passage between islands, but a narrow strip of land (the Isthmus of Panama) joining the two continents of North and South America. The ocean to the West he called the "Southern Sea".

When Balboa reported his discovery to the Spanish Government, there was some talk about cutting a canal through the Isthmus, so that ships could sail directly from the Atlantic into this "Southern Sea". But the task would have been too difficult, in those days before suitable machinery was made, and before doctors found how to prevent and cure malaria. The Panama Canal was not built until 400 years after Balboa's journey across the Isthmus.

Since ships could not enter the "Southern Sea" by sailing due west, it seemed that the only way left was to sail either south, around the South American continent, or north, around the North American continent.

Both ways were tried by later explorers, who still hoped to reach India or China by sailing west, instead of east.

400 years after Balboa, men learned how to control the mosquito by draining swamps, or sometimes filling them in, and by destroying the pupae of the mosquito. Then the Panama Canal was built through the Isthmus, so that ships could pass from the Atlantic Ocean to the Pacific.

DIAZ AND DA GAMA

WHEN King John of Portugal was asked by Columbus to help him with his plan to sail westward across the Atlantic to reach India, the King refused.

"I am too busy," he said. "I have plans of my own for exploring Africa."

Why was King John interested in Africa? It was because his own country, Portugal, was small and had poor soil. King John knew that his people could grow rich only by trading.

In earlier days, the Portuguese had done a good trade with Venice and Genoa, buying from them gold, silk, and spices in exchange for salt, olive oil, and fish. Now this trade had fallen off because of the Turks. The Portuguese had to find new countries to trade with.

Before John, Prince Henry the Navigator had encouraged the seamen of Portugal to explore the west coast of Africa. There they traded in gold, pepper, ivory (from elephants' tusks), and black slaves.

Now King John had a better idea. He wondered if it might be possible to sail right around Africa, and find a new seaway to India. Then his people could trade direct with India and China, without bothering about Venice, Genoa, or the Turks.

You may ask, why did not the Portuguese go overland across Africa on their way to India? That would have been much shorter than going by sea.

But Africa is difficult to cross by land. There are few good harbours on the west coast, where ships can safely land their crews. It is hot and unhealthy. In the centre of the continent lie great deserts, where travellers may die for lack of water. Also, in John's time, the natives of those parts were savage and cruel.

38

1" = 3000 MILES

 Desert

Dry Prairie

Open Grass land with few trees

Damp Jungle

A study of this map with its legend shows why white men did not venture to cross Africa in the early days.

Now look at the map of Africa. At its northern end, near Europe, it is very broad, and bulges out far into the Atlantic. But its southern end is long and narrow, like a thick snout jutting out into the southern ocean. For many hundreds of years no one knew where this snout ended. Or *did* it end at all? Perhaps Africa continued right on to the South Pole!

King John decided to find this out. In 1487, he sent out a fleet of three ships to follow the western coastline of Africa southward to its end. He gave command of this fleet to Bartholomew Diaz, a nobleman who had charge of the King's store-houses. Diaz was well educated, and had studied geography. He was also an experienced seaman.

Diaz had no idea how far he might have to sail to reach the tip of Africa. It might be a thousand miles, or more. He planned to keep in sight of land all the time. But he knew that at any point the winds might blow his ships far out to sea, and make him lose his way. Then he might never get back home.

To mark the route that he took, Diaz carried with him three stone pillars. He planned to set these up, one at a time, at different points on his way along the African coast. The "markers" would help to guide him on his way home. Also, they would show the way to other sailors who might come after him.

Diaz also took some African natives with him. These he planned to land at places along the coast, dressed in fine clothes, so that the savages would think the Portuguese were rich traders. They could take with them small samples of gold and spices, to show the savages what the Portuguese wanted to buy.

Diaz first sailed to the mouth of the Congo River, which was the farthest point south reached by any

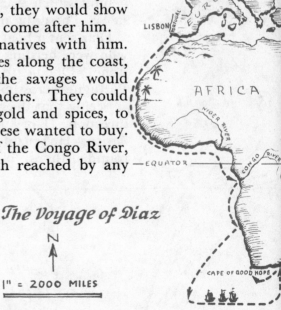

The Voyage of Diaz

N

I" = 2000 MILES

Portuguese seaman before him. Then he began to cruise southward into unknown waters. From the coast hot winds carrying red dust swept over his ships. Diaz found them so uncomfortable that he named this part of the coast "Hell".

Then strong sea currents, flowing north along the coast, slowed the ships down. Diaz landed in a sheltered bay and set up his first marker. Small pieces of this were found not many years ago, and were placed in a museum.

After this Diaz met a fierce gale, lasting thirteen days. The gale blew his fleet far out to the southwest. Diaz did not know it, but in this part of the world the wind always blows steadily in one direction at this time of the year. Afterward seamen called this kind of wind a "trade wind". "Trade" is an old German word meaning *steady*.

When the gale was over, Diaz steered eastward to find the coast again. But he sighted nothing, nothing but endless sea. At last he guessed what this meant.

"We must have passed the southern tip of Africa," Diaz told his officers. "Let us steer northward."

So they sailed northward for nearly 500 miles until they sighted mountains. Diaz anchored in a bay, behind which was a series of grassy hills, rising like steps. These the natives called "karoos".

Diaz sent a boat ashore to get water. Some natives, who were herding cattle there, pelted the sailors with stones. One negro was killed by an arrow shot from a Portuguese crossbow, and the rest fled with their cattle.

Seeing that the coastline now turned in a north-east direction, Diaz knew he must be on the east side of Africa. He set up his second marker, to show he had rounded the tip of the continent and passed from the

EUROPE

AFRICA

EQUATOR

Warm Current ———→
Cold Current ----→
Wind ➤

N

1" = 1600 MILES

Atlantic into the Indian Ocean.

But now his men began to complain about the hardships of the voyage, and begged Diaz to turn back. He persuaded them to sail on for three days more, hoping that by that time they would be willing to go on to India. But they would not change their minds, and Diaz was forced to set up his third marker, and turn his ships toward Portugal again.

On the way home he kept close to the coast, and discovered a high cape jutting out into the ocean at the southern tip of Africa. "I named this the Cape of Torments," he told the King later, "in memory of our troubles during the great storm."

"Let us call it rather the Cape of Good Hope," replied the King, "because it gives us now the hope of reaching India."

And that is the name it bears today.

African Bushman

Vasco da Gama

Soon after the return of Diaz, King John heard that Columbus had crossed the Atlantic, and had found new lands which he called "The Indies". Because Columbus was serving Spain, John became anxious that his own men should reach India before the Spaniards seized it all for themselves. He decided to send out a second Portuguese expedition, to complete the eastern voyage to India and to open up trade with that country. He ordered Diaz to look after the building of four new ships for this purpose.

But before they were ready John died, and the new ruler, King Manuel, placed another nobleman, Vasco da Gama, in command of the expedition. He did this because he thought that an expedition to India needed a commander who was not only a

The natives of South Africa used things ready at hand, reeds and grasses, to build their dwellings. We do the same, but cut trees into boards, make brick from clay, nails from iron, etc.

Negro Village in Natal, South Africa

good navigator, but a warrior. Vasco da Gama had already won fame fighting at sea against the Spaniards.

Diaz built the four ships in a new way. They had two turrets or "castles", one in the bow (fore) and the other at the stern (aft), instead of only one, in the stern. This was to make them stronger for fighting, since both turrets could be filled with soldiers. The word "foc'sle" (short for *forecastle*) has been in use ever since, to describe the front part of any ship.

The ships were not only strong, but roomy. They carried many large sails, to increase their speed, and were manned by 150 men. Among these were some who had been let out of prison, and promised their freedom when they came home if they worked well.

Enough food was carried to last three years. Every day each man could have a pound and a half of ship's biscuit, a pound of salt beef or pork, two and a half pints of water, some olive oil, and wine.

There were also goods on board for trading with the natives—cheap cloth, honey, olive oil, little bells, glass beads, rings, and bracelets made of tin.

Da Gama bade farewell to King Manuel, and prayed with all his men for a successful voyage. In July 1497, with a great crowd looking on, he boarded his flagship, *St. Gabriel*. A second ship, *St. Raphael*, was commanded by his younger brother, Paulo. Diaz sailed with the expedition for part of the journey.

Da Gama remembered what Diaz had said about the ocean currents along the coast of Africa. To escape meeting them, he steered, of his own accord, out into mid-Atlantic. For three months and five days they were out of sight of land. Such a thing had never happened to an expedition before!

They sailed in a wide half circle, until they caught a south-west wind that blew them back to the coast of Africa. On the 6th of November they sighted land and found they were close to the Cape of Good Hope.

Da Gama rounded the Cape in good weather, but then ran into severe storms. His crews became so worn out by the rough weather that they threatened to mutiny unless he turned back. But da Gama was less patient than Diaz had been. He invited the ringleaders into his cabin to talk matters over, had them arrested, and kept them in chains below the ship's deck for the rest of the voyage.

On the 25th of December they sighted land again. Da Gama named it "Natal" because that day was the birthday (or *natal* day) of Christ. Natal today is one of the provinces of the Union of South Africa.

By now da Gama had passed the last marker set up by Diaz, and was exploring a new part of Africa. From time to time he landed, only to find poor villages of mud huts, in which Bantu negroes lived.

But as he sailed farther north, he noticed the natives had paler skins, and lived in stone houses. They were half-Arab, half-negro, and built churches called "mosques", in which they worshipped God in the way taught by Mohammed. These natives were friendly and gave the sailors fresh food, just in time to prevent a bad outbreak of scurvy, a disease caused by lack of vitamins. In spite of this, da Gama lost twenty men from scurvy.

The fleet was now approaching the busy East African towns to which the Arab traders brought their goods. At Mozambique, da Gama found the harbour full of Arab ships, with cargoes of gold, pearls, and spices. These were the very things the

A Moorish building

N

1" = 3000 MILES

ASIA

LISBON

CAPE VERDE IS.

AFRICA

ARABIA

INDIA

CALICUT

EQUATOR

MALINDI

ATLANTIC OCEAN

MOZAMBIQUE

INDIAN OCEAN

NATAL

CAPE OF GOOD HOPE

The Voyage of Vasco da Gama

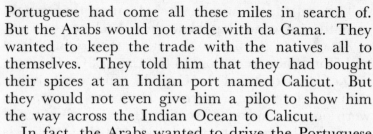

Portuguese had come all these miles in search of. But the Arabs would not trade with da Gama. They wanted to keep the trade with the natives all to themselves. They told him that they had bought their spices at an Indian port named Calicut. But they would not even give him a pilot to show him the way across the Indian Ocean to Calicut.

In fact, the Arabs wanted to drive the Portuguese away from the east coast of Africa altogether. They soon found an excuse for quarrelling with the new-comers, saying they were Christians, and ordering them to weigh anchor and leave Mozambique at once.

At the next place the Portuguese touched, it was worse. The native pilots tried to lead da Gama's ship on to a coral reef and wreck it.

Stranded on a Coral reef

However he pushed on northward to Malindi, where he had better luck. The Sultan, or King, of Malindi had heard that the white men were fearless and dressed all in steel. He thought he would make friends with them, and then ask their help against his enemies. When da Gama had given this help, the Sultan offered him plenty of food, and a good pilot to show him the way to India.

After crossing the Indian Ocean, the Portuguese reached Calicut, on the 20th of May 1498. They were the first Europeans ever to cast anchor in an Indian port. In the country around Calicut the natives grew cotton. Calicut cloth, or calico, takes its name from this port.

The ruler of Calicut was a Hindu prince, wealthy and proud. Richly dressed and covered with jewels, he received da Gama in his palace, and readily gave him permission to trade. But when da Gama brought out his presents for the King, of cheap cloth, honey, beads, and tin bracelets, the King laughed at him.

"Are these the riches of Portugal? We have better goods of our own," he sneered. "You must be pirates, not traders!"

The King was not so friendly with da Gama after this. When da Gama asked where he could get plenty of spices, he was told that spices were not grown in India. He was warned that he would have to go much farther east, to the Moluccas (Spice Islands) if he wished to find their source.

To add to his troubles, the Arab traders in Calicut were jealous of the Portuguese. They made so much trouble for da Gama that, after a time, he thought it wiser to sail for home.

He took on board a cargo of spices and jewels, and a letter from the King of Calicut, written with an iron pen upon a palm leaf. This letter was addressed to King Manuel, and said: "Vasco da Gama, a gentleman of your household, came to my country, whereat I was much pleased. My country is rich in cinnamon, ginger, pepper, and precious stones. That which I ask of you is gold, silver, corals, and scarlet cloth."

The return voyage took a whole year on account of storms, and many of the crew died of scurvy. Paulo da Gama fell ill and died just before they reached home.

As a reward for finding the way by sea to India, King Manuel gave da Gama a title and a thousand pieces of gold. Then he ordered a second expedition of fifteen ships, to be made ready to go to India. Diaz went with this expedition, while da Gama stayed at home.

This fleet, like da Gama's, put out into mid-Atlantic to escape the sea currents off Africa. But it was driven too far to the west, and touched a new land, part of

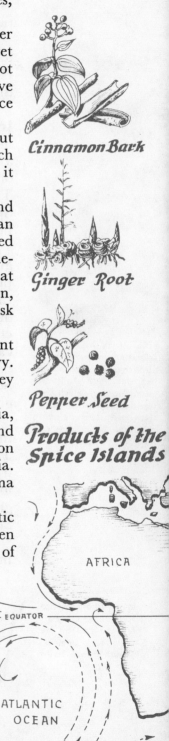

Cinnamon Bark

Ginger Root

Pepper Seed

Products of the Spice Islands

Ocean Currents carried the Portuguese to Brazil

Warm Currents —→
Cold Currents ---→

N

1" = 2250 MILES

AFRICA

EQUATOR

SOUTH AMERICA

ATLANTIC OCEAN

South America. The Portuguese described this land as mountainous and hot, with no opportunities for trading. It was afterwards called Brazil.

The fleet set out from Brazil to complete the voyage to India, but on the way around the Cape of Good Hope some of the ships were lost in a storm. Among these was the ship commanded by Diaz.

Later on da Gama made several more voyages to India, and became Governor of the Portuguese settlements there. From these settlements (or "colonies", as they were called) the Portuguese made attacks on the Arabs and took over their trade with India. The Portuguese then pushed on farther east to the Spice Islands, and even to China. In this way Portugal became the chief market for spices in Europe.

In their hurry to find the way to India, the Portuguese did not trouble to explore fully some of the places they passed. For example, they coasted around the Cape of Good Hope and Natal, without finding out that inland there lay a rich country with a good climate. It was left to the Dutch and English, who came after the Portuguese, to make colonies in this part of South Africa, which is now the Union of South Africa. There oranges and other fruits were grown, and gold and diamonds mined.

The ostrich lives in a dry climate. In South Africa ostriches were once raised for their tail and wing feathers, which were used to trim ladies' hats. Now their skins are made into fine hand-bags and shoes.

Brazil, too, which the Portuguese did not think much of at first, turned out later to be very important. They started a colony there, and found gold, coal, iron, and manganese in its mountains. They also found diamonds in its rivers, and wild rubber trees growing in its jungles. In the deep rich soil of Southern Brazil they were able to grow coffee.

Today, although Brazil is an independent country, most of its people still speak Portuguese.

In addition to rich farmlands, the Portuguese passed by great mineral wealth in their haste to reach India.

☀ *Diamond*
⁙ *Gold*
✦ *Coal*
△ *Iron*
○ *Copper*

Treasures of South Africa

JOHN AND SEBASTIAN CABOT

JOHN CABOT and his son Sebastian lived in Venice, 200 years after the time of Marco Polo. John was both a sailor and a trader. He had travelled to the East more than once to see if he could buy spices to sell in Venice. But one day, when he came home, he had important news for his young son.

"Our trade is bad, Sebastian," he told him. "The Arabs from whom I buy spices hate us Christians so much, and put up the prices so high there is no profit left for us. We must try our luck in a new direction."

"Where are we to go?" asked Sebastian.

"There is a man named Columbus," answered his father, "who says that you can get to Asia, where the spices come from, by sailing due westward from Europe out into the Atlantic. I believe Columbus is right. I intend to do the same."

John and Sebastian Cabot left Venice to pick a new home, where they could try out John's plan for sailing westward. They did not go to Spain, because Columbus had been there before them. Nor did they go to Portugal, because the Portuguese were using their ships to trade with West Africa, or to find a way to India by sailing around the Cape of Good Hope. Instead, they went to England, and settled in Bristol on the west coast. Bristol was the second biggest city in England, and the leading seaport.

Up to this time England had not, like Spain and Portugal, sent seamen to explore new lands. This was mainly due to quarrels inside the country. But at last these quarrels ended, and England became united under a strong and clever king, Henry VII, who wanted to make his country's trade grow faster.

The Matthew

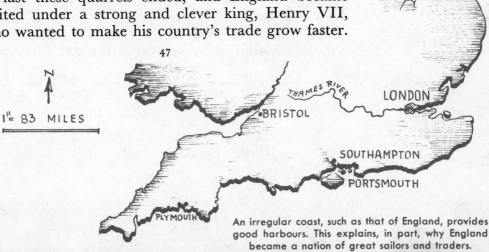

An irregular coast, such as that of England, provides good harbours. This explains, in part, why England became a nation of great sailors and traders.

47

England is a small island-country, with a long coastline. Where the rivers run down to the sea, there are many good harbours for ships. The English climate is mild, because a current of warm water from the Gulf of Mexico passes near her west coast. The meeting of the warm current with the cold water of the North Atlantic causes fog and rain. This rain makes plenty of grass grow in the west and north of England, on which sheep can pasture.

From early times the English had raised sheep, which grew good wool. They sent this wool abroad to many countries, particularly Belgium and Holland. In these countries people were given jobs weaving this wool into cloth. Some of it was used in their own country, and the rest was sold. Some of it was sold to people in England, who found how much more it cost than they had been paid for the wool!

In Henry's time a change was taking place. Instead of sending their wool abroad, the English people learned to weave, and the cloth that they did not need for themselves, they sent abroad and sold. This provided work for English people, and increased the prosperity of the country.

But at first England had very few ships of her own to carry on this trade with other countries. She had to pay the ships and sailors of Venice, Genoa, and other places to do it for her. King Henry thought it would be a good idea to encourage seamen from these places to settle in England. Then they could help his people to build ships and sail them overseas.

So John Cabot had chosen wisely when he picked Bristol as his new home. This city had a good sea trade, not only with Europe, but with Iceland. Probably Cabot met sailors from Iceland, and heard

ICELAND

ATLANTIC OCEAN

SCOTLAND

IRELAND

ENGLAND

Warm Current ———→
Cold Current - - -→
Wool Area

N
↑

1" = 375 MILES

from them Icelandic sagas telling of Leif's voyage to Vineland the Good. These would have made him feel more sure than ever that he could sail direct from England to Asia.

In Bristol there lived many merchants, who thought Cabot's plans were good. If he were able to make his voyage westward, it might bring great wealth to England, and more trade to Bristol, they said. The merchants helped John to get an interview with King Henry.

The King was a shrewd, careful man.

"What do you hope to gain by sailing west, Master Cabot?" he asked.

"I hope to reach Asia, your Majesty," was the reply. "And to find gold and spices, which I will bring back to England."

"But the Spanish and Portuguese are doing the same thing," commented the King. "England is not strong enough to quarrel with them. How do you propose to avoid this?"

"Your Majesty, the Spanish and Portuguese are exploring only the *southern* half of our globe," said John. "I shall keep strictly to the northern half, which is opposite England. There lies the shortest route to Asia, according to my calculations."

King Henry was pleased with John Cabot's answers. He gave him permission to sail under the English flag, and to discover and take possession of any new lands not claimed before by the explorers of any other country. He also promised Cabot a share of the profits of any trade that might come out of his discoveries.

When they knew that the King was favourable, the Bristol merchants helped John to outfit a ship.

ICELAND

ATLANTIC
OCEAN

EUROPE

AFRICA

*English Trading Routes
at the Time of Cabot*

On the 2nd of May 1497, he sailed from Bristol in the *Matthew*, with about eighteen persons on board. Most of the sailors were English, and there were one or two merchants on board who went as passengers, hoping for trade. Sebastian Cabot, who was then fourteen years old, probably sailed with his father, as cabin boy.

After passing Ireland, Cabot steered the *Matthew* northward, then westward across the North Atlantic. The winds were not favourable, and he had often to alter his ship's course. He was at sea for fifty-four days before sighting land.

At last, early on the morning of the 24th of June, Cabot saw two lands. One he thought was an island, which he named St. John, because he had sighted it on St. John's Day. Probably this "island" was the Avalon Peninsula, in the south-east corner of Newfoundland. Cabot thought it was an island, because it was so nearly surrounded by water. Today, the city of St. John's, Newfoundland, stands near the spot where Cabot is said to have seen land.

The English were impressed with the amazing quantity of fish in the shallow seas around St. John. There were sturgeon, salmon, and, above all, codfish. "You could catch them in hundreds, not only with a net, but just by letting down a basket with a stone in it," so Cabot told his friends after his return home.

The other land that Cabot saw was a coastline, which he took to be the mainland of Asia. However, on closer view, this land did not look at all like Marco Polo's China or Japan. It was a wild, barren country, inhabited by savages dressed in furs and skins. The English saw there bears and moose and many kinds of birds.

N

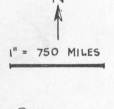

1" = 750 MILES

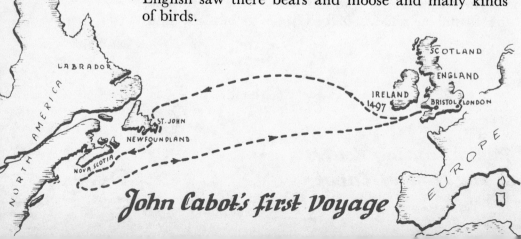

John Cabot's first Voyage

Probably this coast was another part of Newfoundland, farther west than St. John's. Here John Cabot landed, and took possession of the new country by unfurling the flag of England. But he did not stay there long, because his men were too few to face the risk of a fight with the savages.

After this, he sailed along the coast for about three weeks. We do not know exactly what places he visited. He may have landed at other places on Newfoundland, and later have crossed to Cape Breton Island and coasted along Nova Scotia. At any rate he was the first explorer since the Norsemen to reach the mainland of North America, and to land on the east coast of Canada.

By mid-July Cabot was running short of food, and so started on his return journey. This time he had a quick passage with favourable winds. The *Matthew* sailed into Bristol on the 6th of August, with all her crew safe and sound.

John went quickly up to London, to report to King Henry.

"I have found what is probably Asia, your Majesty," he said, not realizing it was North America he had seen. "I have brought back neither gold nor spices, but there is enough fish in the seas there to feed all England."

King Henry did not seem to care much about fish. But he rewarded Cabot with a gift of money, gave him a pension for life, and suggested he make a second voyage to the New World.

The Bristol merchants were again willing to help, so next year John Cabot was given command of a fleet of four or five vessels, for one of which the King himself paid. They sailed from Bristol in May 1498.

There are no records to show what happened on this voyage. It seems not to have been as successful as the first. Possibly John Cabot was drowned at sea, or, if he came back to England, died soon afterward.

His son, Sebastian, grew up to be an explorer like his father. By this time, the discoveries of Columbus and Balboa and others had shown that you could not reach Asia direct by sailing due west across the Atlantic. There was something big lying in the way —not Japan, but a new continent, America. Sebastian suspected that the land his father and he had seen on their first voyage must have been part of this new continent. But if so, it had no spices or gold. Was there a way around, or through this continent?

Sebastian had a bright idea. What if he steered farther north than his father had done? Would he find a passage or strait leading past the new continent? That might bring him, in the end, to Asia, the land of spices and gold!

The merchants of Bristol helped him to get ready two ships, and Sebastian set sail early in the spring of 1509. The farther north he went, the longer the days became. At last he reached a point where the sun did not set, and there was no night at all. On the other hand, the sea was growing colder and colder, and was covered with masses of drifting ice.

From the map Sebastian has left us, it appears that he sailed up the west coast of Greenland, and into what is now called Davis Strait. On his return, he probably noticed an opening which leads westward into Hudson Bay, and wondered if it were the passage to Asia he was looking for.

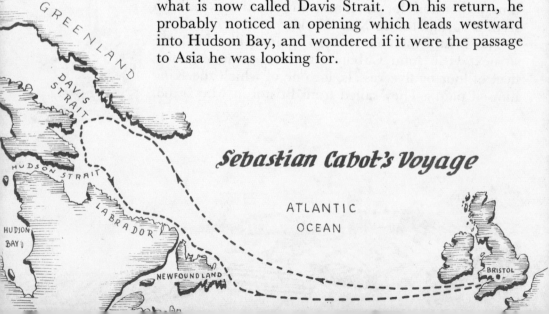

Sebastian Cabot's Voyage

But at this point, either his courage failed him, or his men mutinied. He appears to have turned south, coasted along Labrador to Newfoundland, and then started for home.

When he reached Bristol he found that King Henry VII was dead, and that the Bristol merchants would not give him aid for another expedition. So Sebastian went off to Spain and other countries, to offer his services there and try to interest people in his idea of a north-west route to the East. But he had little success and, from time to time, he went back to England.

Gradually the English people were beginning to think that gold and spices were not the only things worth exploring for. Newfoundland might, after all, be very important to England. Fleets were outfitted and sent to fish in the shallow waters (known as the Grand Banks) near Newfoundland. They brought back cargoes of dried and salted cod, which were sold to Spain, Portugal, and other lands bordering on the Mediterranean Sea. Fish did not cost so much as meat, and when it had been dried and salted, it did not spoil. It made good food for people living in warm climates.

Now that the people of Europe could get dried fish to eat, they were not so anxious to have spices to keep their meats tasty. So the water route across the North Atlantic became, in time, a more important trade route than the eastern route to Asia.

But people did not forget about finding a sea route to Asia. Some people thought that, if John Cabot had been right about the wealth of Newfoundland, Sebastian might also be right about the "passage" that he said he had seen on his voyage to the North

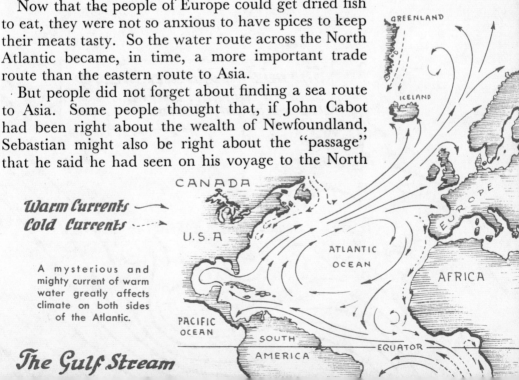

Warm Currents ⟶
Cold Currents ⤏

A mysterious and mighty current of warm water greatly affects climate on both sides of the Atlantic.

The Gulf Stream

West. Had he really seen the entrance to a new ocean, leading on to China? Should an attempt be made to explore this North-West Passage?

Sebastian Cabot was now too old to make more voyages. On his advice, one or two small expeditions were sent out to search for the Passage. But they failed to find anything.

Then it was suggested that perhaps the Passage might lie in a different direction. Perhaps you could get to Asia by sailing *north-east*, around the north of Europe?

Sebastian was a member of a committee that managed an expedition in search of a North-East Passage. This voyage opened up new trade with Russia, but no way to the East was found.

"I still believe in the North-West Passage to Asia," Sebastian Cabot kept on saying.

Many English explorers who came after him believed that Sebastian was right.

The mixing of warm and cold water masses over a rather shallow part of the Atlantic Ocean, called the Grand Banks, makes conditions favourable to the growing of tiny sea animals and plants (a food for some kinds of fish). Because of this, the Grand Banks have been one of the world's greatest fishing grounds since Cabot's time.

The mixing of water masses
The cold Labrador Current ----▶
The warm Gulf Stream ━━▶

LABRADOR

NEWFOUNDLAND

GRAND BANKS

NOVA SCOTIA

THE WORLD'S
BIGGEST OCEAN

MAGELLAN

WHEN King Manuel welcomed Vasco da Gama home to Lisbon from India, the King had with him a young lad of eighteen, named Ferdinand Magellan. Ferdinand had served the King since boyhood, but did not seem well suited for court life. Though strong and active, he was too silent and quick-tempered to win the royal favour.

Seeing da Gama's success, Ferdinand made up his mind to become an explorer too. The King gave him permission to leave the court and go to sea. Naturally Magellan wanted to sail east, because everyone knew that da Gama's voyage was only a first step, and that all the wealth of the Indies was now waiting to be brought home to Portugal.

The young seaman was away from home for seven years in the East, and during that time he had plenty of adventure. First, he took part in several battles with the Arabs, who had to be cleared out of the way before the Portuguese could develop their trade with India. Next, the Portuguese pushed on beyond India

55

to capture from the Arabs the Spice Islands. To reach
these, their ships had to pass through a narrow sea-
passage, called the Strait of Malacca.

Magellan was twice wounded in battle. Once he
saved his Admiral's life. Once he put down a dangerous mutiny among his fellow seamen. For this he was
promoted to be captain of a ship. Lastly, after taking
part in the capture of Malacca, he returned home to
Lisbon.

There he did not get along as well as he had hoped.
King Manuel thought he was too proud and independent. When Magellan asked the King to raise
his pay a little, his request was refused. This touched
his pride.

"It seems, Sire," he said, "that I no longer enjoy
your Majesty's favour. May I leave Lisbon and go to
seek my fortune with some other master, who will like
me better?"

"You may go anywhere you please."

Manuel was glad to get rid of Magellan. He even
refused to let the young captain kiss his royal hand at
parting.

Feeling deeply hurt, Magellan left Portugal at once.
went to Spain, and became a citizen of that country.

While he was away in the East, Magellan had kept
himself well informed about what other explorers were
doing. He knew that the Spaniards, after Columbus
had made his voyage, had opened up the Islands of
the Caribbean Sea for trading, and had landed on the
mainland of North America, at Florida and Panama.
He knew that Balboa had crossed the mainland at a
place where it was very narrow, and had found on the
other side of it the "Southern Sea". He also knew
that another great mainland had been discovered to

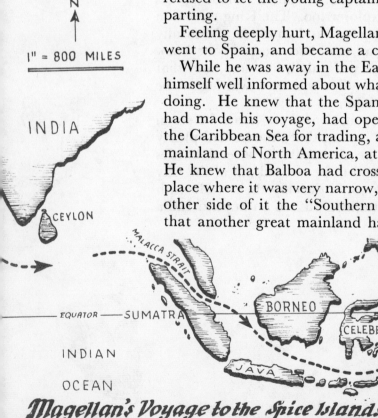

Magellan's Voyage to the Spice Islands

the south, and that seamen had sailed down its
eastern coast as far as Brazil.

But no one yet knew how large these mainlands
were, or whether they were surrounded by sea at the
north and south ends.

Magellan guessed that there could be no direct
water-way between the two mainlands, leading to the
southern ocean. If that were true, then the only way
to reach India by sailing west, would be to go either
south-west, around the tip of the southern mainland
(South America), or north-west around the tip of the
northern mainland (North America). Magellan had
heard that the King of England had already sent
navigators (John and Sebastian Cabot) to find the
North-West Passage. Why should not he find the
South-West Passage to the Southern Sea?

With this idea in his head, Magellan approached
the young King of Spain, Charles, and asked him to
provide ships and men to discover this southern route.

"If I do find a way into the Southern Sea," he told
the King, "I will sail westward across it, and reach the
Spice Islands."

"What good will that do?" asked Charles. "The
Spice Islands have already been reached by the
Portuguese, and the trade in spices belongs to them."

"But, your Majesty, Spain is stronger than Portugal," replied Magellan. "Your men can easily take
the spice trade away from the Portuguese."

King Charles did not like this advice. Only
recently, Spain and Portugal had come to a friendly
agreement to divide the New World equally between
them. The Spice Islands were part of Portugal's share,
and King Charles had no wish to go to war with King
Manuel about the matter.

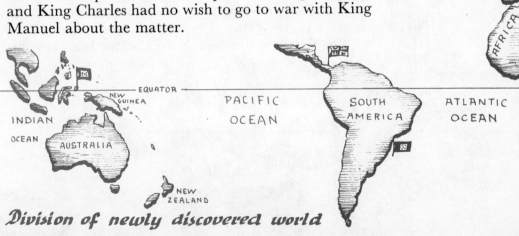

Division of newly discovered world

However a bishop at the court of Charles remembered how Spain had delayed in sending out Columbus, and how nearly she had missed the chance to discover the New World. He spoke to King Charles and urged him to give Magellan better treatment.

The King then gave way, and promised Magellan five ships. He was to search for a south-west passage into the Southern Sea, and then explore for new islands. The King promised him a share in the profits of trading with any new islands he could find.

While the ships were being outfitted, news of the expedition reached King Manuel of Portugal. Manuel was very angry, and sent a message to his Ambassador at the Spanish court, telling him to offer Magellan money, if he would return to Lisbon. But this Magellan refused to do.

Then the Ambassador was ordered to stir up trouble for Magellan among the captains of his ships. This was easy to do, for two reasons. Magellan was a stern commander, and not popular with his men. Also, he was a Portuguese by birth. His captains, who were Spaniards, did not like being led by a foreigner. So even before the expedition started, the seeds of mutiny were sown. For instance, Magellan had ordered that enough food should be taken for two years, but provisions enough for only one year were put on board.

On the 20th of September 1519, the five ships sailed from Seville, in Spain. Magellan sailed on the flagship, the *Trinidad*. He had invented a new system of signalling, to make sure that all his other ships followed his orders by day and by night. But it was not long before he noticed that one of his captains was taking no notice of these signals. Magellan at once replaced him by his own cousin, whom he could trust.

The fleet first touched at the Canary Islands (which

Taking on provisions and water from small ships

belonged to Spain) to take in fresh water. Then it sailed some distance southward along the African coast, till it caught the trade winds blowing due west. These winds carried the fleet across the Atlantic to Brazil, where it arrived about Christmas time.

After a short stay there, to repair the ships and take in more water, the Spaniards continued southward along the east coast of South America. They came to a large bay which Magellan thought might be the passage to the west that they were looking for. However he found that the tides there were not like ocean tides, so he decided that this bay must be only the mouth of a great river. After exploring this river, which was afterward called La Plata, for some distance, Magellan returned to the Atlantic, and pushed on farther south.

The ships were now in the southern half of the globe, where the seasons were changed about. In February, summer ended and winter set in. The days grew shorter and the weather colder, and they were troubled by thick fogs and bitter winds.

The ships put in to a sheltered harbour, the Bay of St. Julian, where Magellan decided to spend the winter. The land around was bleak and rocky, rising to high, snow-capped mountains (the Andes). The inhabitants were Indians, who hunted game with a kind of lassoo made of two stones tied together with a leather thong. The Spaniards called these Indians "patagons", or giants, because they were taller than ordinary men. Their country has ever since been known as Patagonia.

At St. Julian the food supply of the Spanish fleet ran short. Magellan had to put his crews on short rations, which made them grumble. This was the moment the trouble-makers had been waiting for.

A Patagonian

EQUATOR

BRAZIL

LA PLATA

PACIFIC OCEAN

ATLANTIC OCEAN

ST. JULIAN

STRAIT OF MAGELLAN

Magellan's Voyage ....
The cold West Drift --------
The warm Equatorial Current ⌐

N

1" = 900 MILES

On Easter Sunday three of the five ships mutinied. But Magellan acted quickly. He sent a party of his sailors to one of the mutinous ships, the *Victoria*, to ask its captain to come over and see him on the *Trinidad*.

"I am not to be caught like that," laughed Mendoza, when he read the invitation. These were his last words. The next moment, at Magellan's order, the messengers plunged their daggers into his throat! This bold act broke the back of the mutiny.

Magellan hanged one of his captains, and put another on shore to fend for himself as best he could. The rest of the mutineers he pardoned.

This was not the last piece of misfortune. One ship was destroyed in the storm, although its crew and stores were saved. Grumbling still went on among the men, and Magellan was glad when good weather came and the four ships could continue their voyage south.

Before long they sighted a great cape, jutting out far to the east, with mountains from which smoke issued. This cape was separated by a wide channel of water from the mainland. The sailors called it "Tierra del Fuego" (Land of Fire) because of its smoking volcanoes.

Magellan wondered if this channel might be the mouth of another great river leading inland. He sent the two smaller ships of his fleet ahead to explore it, and followed more slowly with the two larger. Soon the lookout man on the *Trinidad* saw the "scouts" returning with flags flying and guns booming.

"This is not a river, Captain-General," the men declared. "The water is salt, and the channel grows broader the farther inland we go."

"Then," cried Magellan, "it must be the gateway to the Southern Sea!"

SOUTH
AMERICA

ATLANTIC OCEAN

PACIFIC
OCEAN

STRAITS OF MAGELLAN

TIERRA
DEL
FUEGO

CAPE HORN

The winding and dangerous channel through which Magellan threaded his way is almost continuously buffeted by storms and high winds. The pictures on this and the opposite page convey some idea of the hazards of the voyage.

Magellan was right, although it took many weeks to prove it. Every step of their way was through unknown waters, and along a narrow channel that wound through high, snow-crowned mountains.

They had to search every inlet, and avoid rocks and dangerous currents. They were lashed by icy winds and attacked by fierce storms. All the time they were on short rations, and dared not land anywhere for fear of the Indians.

The four ships became separated, and one of them deserted and sailed home to Spain. Magellan called a council of officers on the remaining three ships, to decide whether to go forward, or turn back. His determination won the day, and all agreed to push on through the Passage. Ever since then this channel has borne his name—the "Straits of Magellan".

After sailing over 300 miles, the way opened before them. On the 28th of November 1520, the little fleet, sailing under a midnight sun (for there was almost no night at midsummer, so far south) steered out boldly north-west into the ocean that no white men had ever before navigated!

Now began one of the most terrible journeys ever recorded. The Spaniards had no idea how large this ocean was. It was about three times as large as the Atlantic. Although it is full of islands, most of them are small, so it is possible to sail 1,500 miles across it without sighting land!

Magellan sailed for ninety-eight days without seeing anything except two barren islands. His sailors had no food left. They could catch few fish, because fish are not found in great numbers except where they can get food—that is, in fairly shallow water. Instead, the sailors gnawed chips of wood, swallowed scraps of leather from the rigging, and caught and ate the ship's

rats. The water on board turned yellow and smelly, and had to be doled out by the ounce. Scurvy broke out and plagued the men with boils, killing nineteen of them. Yet most of the time they sailed under a hot sun, over such a calm sea that Magellan called it the "Pacific Ocean"—*pacific* is a Latin word, meaning "peaceful".

On the 5th of March, nineteen months after leaving Spain, they came to one of the Ladrones Islands. Magellan named it "Isle of Thieves", because the natives stole one of his boats, although they let the sailors have pigs and vegetables to eat.

Ten days later, the Spaniards reached one of the Philippine Islands, and Magellan thought he was near his goal. Dark-skinned, frizzy-haired natives brought the strangers nutmeg, mace, and other spices, which they said were plentiful in near-by islands. They gave the sailors coconuts, and explained that they could use them to make bread, wine, and oil. From the husks, they could make ropes, and from the shells, cups.

The next island looked even more promising. The Spaniards marvelled at the signs of plenty on every side. The natives wore gold ornaments, and feasted off rice and pork. The climate was very warm, and the soil fertile and well-watered with monsoon rains. On the shore grew tangled shrubs called mangroves, and inland were thick forests of evergreens. In these were found birds of paradise and parrots.

Magellan had with him a native slave, Henry, whom he had brought home with him from his first voyage to the Far East. Henry recognized the speech of these people, and was able to talk with them. This pleased Magellan greatly, because it proved that he had succeeded in his object of sailing around the world.

Bird of Paradise

In summer, the land is warmer than the sea. The air over the land rises and moist sea air flows in, bringing rain. In winter, the opposite is true.

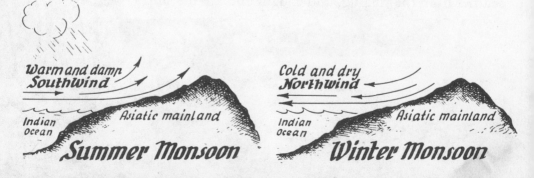

Warm and damp Southwind

Indian Ocean

Asiatic mainland

Summer Monsoon

Cold and dry Northwind

Indian Ocean

Asiatic mainland

Winter Monsoon

He had reached a point by sailing *west*, that the Portuguese had arrived at by sailing *east*.

Magellan's greatest triumph came when he reached Sebu, one of the largest and richest of the Philippines. Here the native king, who had already done business with Portuguese traders, agreed not only to open up trade with the Spaniards, but to become Christian, with all his people. Magellan, who was a very pious man, himself baptized the King and 800 of his people, and ordered them to destroy their native gods.

At this point success seems to have turned Magellan's head. There was a small island close to Sebu, named Mactan, whose ruler refused to follow the example of the King of Sebu, and submit to Spain. Magellan decided to punish the ruler of Mactan by a display of Spanish valour. Against the advice of the King of Sebu, he took eighty of his men, clad in full armour, and tried to capture Mactan by surprise.

But the natives had been warned. They fell upon the Spaniards in thousands and overwhelmed them by force of numbers. Magellan himself was cut off, and killed at the water's edge. His men fled in confusion to their ships.

When he saw that white men could be defeated in battle, the King of Sebu changed his mind, and gave up Christianity. The native slave, Henry, turned traitor, and advised the King to invite Magellan's officers to a feast, and then attack them when they were eating. This was done, and most of the Spanish officers were killed.

The Spanish ships, now reduced to two, sailed away to Borneo, and from there, after months of wandering, reached the Moluccas, or Spice Islands. There they met with a friendly reception, and took on board a

Articles made from the Coconut

Burial of Magellan

cargo of cloves and other spices. But one of the two ships, the *Trinidad*, was found to be so leaky that she had to be abandoned. Only the *Victoria*, with less than fifty Spaniards on board, was left to make the homeward voyage to Spain.

On the 8th of September 1522, she cast anchor at Seville, almost three years after she had set out. It was a sad home-coming, since Magellan himself, the greatest navigator of his time, and the hero of the voyage, was not there to share in the triumph.

And for Spain herself, the triumph was not very great. Magellan had found a way for Spanish ships to enter the Pacific Ocean, and to reach the Spice Islands by sailing westward. But the Straits named after him (the narrow passage he had found through the southern tip of the South American continent) were difficult and dangerous to navigate. Not many sailors dared to make such a voyage. No fleets of trading vessels followed Magellan's course, as they had followed Columbus and da Gama.

The Philippine Islands became a Spanish colony, and each year Spanish ships went there to trade, during the season of the north-east winds. They started from a port on the west coast of Mexico, to avoid going through the Straits of Magellan.

In fact, the next important seaman to thread his way through these dangerous waters, was an Englishman, Francis Drake. That was nearly sixty years later, and Drake came, not to help Spain's trade, but to destroy it!

Magellan's terrible voyage had proved one thing, however. That was, that a ship could sail around the globe in one direction, and return safely to the same point from which it had started. Now people had a more exact idea of the size of the Pacific Ocean.

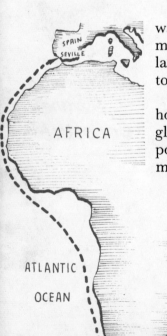

N

1" = 1600 MILES

SPAIN
SEVILLE

AFRICA

INDIAN
OCEAN

ATLANTIC

OCEAN

SUMATRA

BORNEO

JAVA

PHILIPPINE IS.

SEBU

MINDANAO

CELEBES

MOLUCCAS

AUSTRALIA

Return Voyage of the last of Magellan's ships

DRAKE

ONE morning, nearly 400 years ago, a side-door in the palace of Queen Elizabeth I of England opened, to let in a visitor. He did not look like a subject coming to pay his respects to Her Majesty. He seemed more like a friend, called in to advise on secret but importance business.

The visitor was a thickly-built man, with reddish beard, round face, and a keen, cheerful look in his eyes. He was Francis Drake, a bold captain from Devon, who had made a name for himself by raiding the Spanish settlements in the New World. Drake was admired in England, but the Spaniards called him a "pirate".

Queen Elizabeth needed Captain Drake's help. She received him in a friendly way, and spoke to him more as if she were talking to her brother, than giving orders to one of her subjects.

"Drake," she said, "I would gladly be revenged on the King of Spain for divers injuries that I have received."

Why did the Queen want revenge? What injuries had she received from Philip II, the King of Spain?

At this time Spain was the richest and most powerful country in the world. She had colonies in Mexico and Central America, and claimed all of South America, except Brazil. The Spaniards had found rich silver mines in Northern Mexico, and gold mines in the mountains (Andes) of Peru, in South America. Each year the gold was brought down from the mountains to Callao, the port of Lima, and taken by ship to Panama. There it was sent overland on the backs of mules and llamas (a kind of camel) to the

Llama

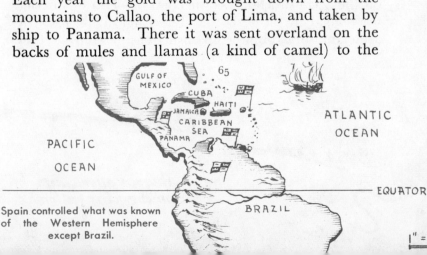

65

GULF OF MEXICO
CUBA
JAMAICA   HAITI
CARIBBEAN SEA
PANAMA

ATLANTIC OCEAN

PACIFIC OCEAN

SPAIN

AFRICA

EQUATOR

BRAZIL

N

Spain controlled what was known of the Western Hemisphere except Brazil.

1" = 1600 MILES

Atlantic Ocean, loaded onto big Spanish galleons, and shipped to Spain. King Philip got most of his money from this source.

England had as yet made few discoveries, and had gained no colonies. She had not even followed up John Cabot's voyage, by making a settlement on Newfoundland. However she sent her fishing fleets to the Grand Banks, and English seamen were already becoming famous for their boldness and skill as traders.

Naturally, English seamen wanted to trade with the Spanish settlements in America. They wanted to exchange English wool and cloth for Spanish gold and silver. But the King of Spain insisted that all trade of this kind be carried on only by his subjects and in his ships.

However there was one kind of goods that the Spanish settlers needed badly, and that was labour. The Spaniards had treated the American Indians so cruelly that a great many of them died, and there were not enough Indians left to work the mines and cotton plantations of the New World.

The British traders began capturing negroes on the west coast of Africa, shipping them across the Atlantic, and offering them for sale as slaves to the Spanish settlers. Although King Philip forbade the settlers to buy, they could not resist the offer. So an unlawful trade in slaves with the English sprang up and went on for several years.

Indians, working for the Spaniards

Of course this led to trouble. The Spaniards often attacked English trading-vessels when they appeared off the Spanish Main (as the coast of Central America was called in those days). The English hit back by attacking and robbing Spanish treasure ships as they

Negros, working on the plantations

crossed the Atlantic. Many sea-fights took place, in which the English "sea-dogs" usually had the best of it, because their ships were lighter and faster than the clumsy Spanish galleons.

Drake had taken part in some of these fights, and had captured many Spanish ships. This made King Philip so angry, that he sent messages to Elizabeth warning her to "stop this Master Thief of the Western World". The Queen was afraid that Philip intended to attack and conquer England, as soon as he had enough ships and gold. That was why she had sent for Captain Drake to strike another blow for her in the "Spanish Main".

"I have to be careful," she explained to Drake. "Spain is more powerful than England still, and I do not wish to provoke Philip to attack me until I am ready. I want to weaken him first."

"I understand your Majesty very well," replied Drake. "If something can be done to stop the flow of gold and silver from the New World into Spain, then King Philip will not be able to carry out his plans for attacking England."

The Queen and Drake quickly worked out a plan of action. Drake was to set out on a peaceful trading expedition. He was to pass through the Straits discovered by Magellan fifty years before, and to explore the Pacific Ocean. His voyage, however, was to take him not directly across the Pacific to the Spice Islands, but up the west coast of South America to the Spanish settlements in Peru and Panama. When he reached these places, he was to do all he could to interfere with Spain's treasure-trade, but without giving Philip cause to declare war on England.

The Queen helped Drake to get the ships he wanted,

Spanish treasure-ship pursued by lighter English vessel

and also paid part of the cost of outfitting them. She hoped she would get this money back, if Drake succeeded. But she urged him to keep very quiet about his voyage, first, because some of her own advisers were against it, and second, because Philip had many spies in England. So Drake told his crew that he was sailing east, to buy currants in Egypt.

On the 17th of November 1577, five ships sailed from Plymouth, in Devon. The largest was the *Pelican*, Drake's flagship, which carried 20 guns. There were 164 seamen on board, and a number of young men of wealth and good birth who wanted to share in the adventure. These young gentlemen knew nothing of the sea, but Drake ordered them to work like the sailors, and share all their hardships.

The voyage began gaily. The *Pelican* was fitted up in grand style, with fine furniture in the cabin and silver dishes in the kitchen. There were four musicians to play during Drake's dinner. The Captain held prayers twice a day, and often addressed his officers and men. As soon as they were safely away from England, he told them that their real destination was the Pacific.

Following Magellan's course, Drake sailed into Port St. Julian near the end of June. On the desolate shore of Patagonia the men could see the remains of a gallows—the one set up by Magellan to hang one of his rebellious captains.

Unfortunately, Drake was forced to do the same thing. One of the gentlemen, who had been causing trouble throughout the voyage, was brought to trial. Drake acted as judge, and forty seamen made up the jury. The offender was found guilty of mutiny, and beheaded.

As it was hard to keep five ships together on a long

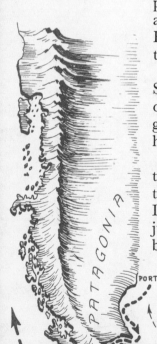

PATAGONIA

PORT ST. JULIAN

FALKLAND IS.

ATLANTIC OCEAN

COLD CURRENT

CAPE HORN

Drake discovers Cape Horn

voyage, Drake left two of his ships behind, when entering the Straits of Magellan. In less than three weeks, he threaded the dangerous passage and came out into the Pacific Ocean. There he changed the name of his flagship to the *Golden Hind*, to put off the track any Spaniards who might have heard of his voyages. But then a fierce gale drove his three ships southward. One of them was sunk with all hands. Another lost touch with Drake and returned to London. Only the *Golden Hind* was left.

She was blown far to the south. Then the gale died away, and Drake caught sight of a great headland, shaped like a horn. Cape Horn, as he called it, was the southern tip of the South American continent.

Drake had found a new way of passing from the Atlantic Ocean into the Pacific. This route around Cape Horn, in spite of the fierce storms that always rage there, was safer than Magellan's Straits. It was used by trading ships until the opening of the Panama Canal.

Drake now steered north-west, until he sighted the coast of Chile, and the high mountains of the Andes. Along the southern part of this coast the rainfall was good. Between the mountains ran valleys covered with grass and scrub, where flocks of sheep and goats pastured.

Farther north, however, the mountains rose higher, and the hot winds blowing off the sea carried their moisture farther inland. Here the coast valleys were dry and barren, good for growing crops only where water could be brought down from the mountains.

On the 5th of November Drake sailed into a bay where there was a valley, facing north, that received plenty of rain, and was very fertile. The Spaniards

Moist air from the Pacific Ocean is forced upward by the Andes Mountains, is cooled, and the moisture falls as rain. The wind then passing over Argentina carries little moisture.

Moist air
Pacific Ocean
Andes
Dry air
Argentina
Atlantic Ocean

called it Valparaiso, or "Paradise Valley", and had
built a settlement there. Drake attacked this, and
took his first prize, a treasure-ship with 1,100 pounds
of gold on board. This gold had been dug out of
mines in the Andes, in Central Peru, and was now on
its way to Spain. The Spaniards had no idea that any
English ship would dare enter the Pacific, and so had
not fortified the harbour.

Drake continued his course along the bleak coast,
with its snow-capped mountains, and showed his
daring by taking the *Golden Hind* right into Callao
harbour one evening. He anchored in the midst of
the Spanish fleet, pretending that the *Golden Hind* was
a Spanish merchantman. After dark he stealthily
boarded a neighbouring ship, the *San Cristobal*, and
captured her. But during the scuffle his secret was
discovered. The alarm was given, and all the armed
forces of Lima and Callao turned out to beat off the
attack—which, they thought, came from pirates or
Indians. But by the time they were ready to fight,
Drake had slipped out to sea taking his prize with him.
Her cargo was mainly of silk and linen, brought from
Europe to trade with the Spanish settlers.

Drake's secret could not be kept any longer—but
his greatest deed was yet to come. He gave chase to
Our Lady of the Conception, a treasure-ship known to the
Spaniards as "the glory of the South Seas". Again he
pretended to be a Spanish merchant-ship, until he
was alongside of his prey.

The Spanish captain called upon Drake to sur-
render. The reply was a chain-shot from one of the
Golden Hind's guns that crippled the Spanish ship. The
Spanish captain was wounded, and his crew taken
prisoner. Four hundred thousand *pesos* of gold and

silver were taken from *Our Lady of the Conception.* This would be worth nearly $10,000,000 in our money today. Drake invited the wounded Spanish captain to dinner, treated him well, and presented him with some armour and weapons, to remind him of his encounter with the *Golden Hind!*

This region was now becoming too dangerous for Drake to stay in. How was he to get home? He believed if he tried to return to England by the Straits of Magellan, or by Cape Horn, the Spaniards would be waiting for him. Instead, he decided to try to discover a passage to the Atlantic around the north of North America.

Drake never found this passage. He had to turn back on account of bitter cold and thick fogs. But he touched a point on the west coast not far from present-day San Francisco. There he repaired his ship, and received presents of tobacco from the Indians. He named the country New Albion, and noted that the climate there was warm, and the rainfall good. Albion was an old name for England.

Drake now sailed due west and crossed the Pacific Ocean to the Philippine Islands in sixty-eight days. There he took in water for his ship, and hurried on to the Spice Islands. Drake had planned to capture the spice trade from the Portuguese. Luckily he found a friend in the Sultan of Ternate, the northermost of these islands. This Sultan hated the Portuguese, and so was ready to do business with the English. Drake bought from him six tons of cloves, paying for them with the silks and linens taken from the *San Cristobal.*

As the *Golden Hind* continued her voyage through the East Indian Islands, she was a treasure-ship herself, carrying only fifty-eight men, but packed with

Stranded on a coral reef

gold, silver, and spices. One night Drake was running his ship under full sail before a steady breeze, when she struck a reef and was held there, helpless. The crew gave the ship up for lost, but Drake's courage did not falter. All hands were called to attend communion service and hear a sermon. Then, to lighten the ship, half her precious cargo of spices, several of her guns, and some of her provisions were dumped overboard. The ship, being now lighter, slid off the reef and miraculously floated. They were saved!

Drake stayed for two weeks at Java, an island with volcanoes, lakes, and evergreen forests. The soil, formed of lava from the volcanoes, was good, and in the coastal plains and the valleys where the rainfall was heavy, rice was raised.

After leaving Java, the *Golden Hind* crossed the Indian Ocean, rounded the Cape of Good Hope, and touched at Sierra Leone on the west coast of Africa. In October 1580 the little ship anchored at Plymouth, having taken two years and ten months, and some few odd days, in sailing round the world!

Drake was not sure what sort of welcome he would get in England. Would the Spanish Ambassador demand his head, as a penalty for his raids on Spanish shipping?

The Queen, after a private talk with Drake, had no doubts. She had his treasure counted, valued, and stored away. It included twenty tons of silver, five blocks of gold (each 18 inches long), and many pearls and diamonds. The total value today would be £5,000,000, or about $15,000,000. For every dollar the Queen and her courtiers had lent Drake to outfit his expedition, they received at least fourteen from the profits of the voyage. No wonder the Queen rewarded

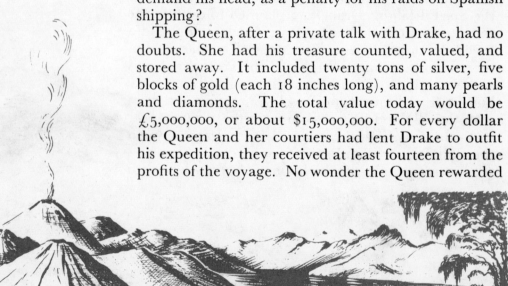

Volcanoes on Java

Drake with a knighthood, making him "Sir Francis Drake". She also let him keep for himself about $50,000 of the treasure he had brought home.

The loss of his treasure-ships made King Philip of Spain poorer, and delayed for several years his invasion of England. In the meantime, Queen Elizabeth used the treasure Drake had brought home to strengthen her fleet. This fleet easily defeated the Spanish Armada (Great Fleet) when it did come.

After this, Spain ceased to be a powerful Empire. But English seamen began to make regular trading voyages across the Atlantic, and in time established settlements on the east coast of North America.

Because Drake had found a safe way for ships around Cape Horn, the Pacific Ocean was now open to navigators of all countries. With the rivalry for trade in spices and other products, more and more of this great ocean was explored, and its many islands, now shown on your map, gradually discovered.

Drake's Voyage around the World, 1577-1580

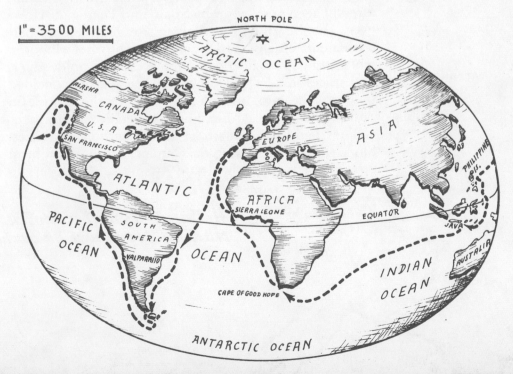

TASMAN

DRAKE'S voyage around the world, by weakening Spain, helped another country besides his own. Across the North Sea to the east lay Holland. In Drake's time, this country was under the rule of Spain. Many of the Spanish overlords were cruel, and the Dutch people were fighting to gain their freedom. When England defeated the Armada in 1588, Spain was no longer strong enough to rule Holland, and the Dutch people declared their independence.

Holland was a small, flat, low country. In fact, the people had to build dikes to prevent the sea from flooding their land. It is not surprising that they were good sailors. As soon as their country became independent they began to live by trading overseas. They built a fleet of ships which carried cargoes of linen from Germany, and salt from the Cape Verde Islands, to the New World. Soon Dutch ships were trading all over the world, and bringing great wealth home to their native land.

The next step for the Dutch was to explore new lands, and make trading settlements in them. But they found that the best parts of the New World had already been opened up by Spain and Portugal. However, the Spanish and Portuguese had made their settlements chiefly in the countries with hot climates, where they thought the greatest wealth in gold, silver, and spices lay. The Dutch, like the English, decided to push on, into unexplored parts of the world, in South Africa, the Arctic, and the Pacific Ocean.

They had their first stroke of luck in the East Indies. Since the days of Vasco da Gama, Portugal had been growing rich from the trade in spices. However, to

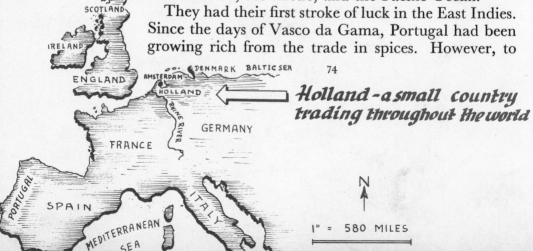

Holland - a small country trading throughout the world

1" = 580 MILES

gain this trade she had had to make long voyages, and spend a great deal of money building trading-posts in the Far East. Besides, those in charge of the industry became so rich that they grew lazy. Often they were cruel to the natives, who then began to dislike having them there. At last the Portuguese found it hard to hold the places they had discovered—especially the Spice Islands. The Dutch slipped in and took over for themselves the rich trade in spices. To manage this trade, a group of merchants formed the Dutch East India Company. So well did it succeed that, in a few years, Holland became a great world power.

Van Diemen, the Governor of the Dutch islands in the East Indies, had the idea of extending Dutch trade still further, by exploring the South Seas of the Pacific Ocean. He knew that Magellan and Drake had sailed across the Pacific and found several new islands. But it was clear that this vast ocean must hold other lands, perhaps of greater size and importance. People even spoke of a great land stretching away far to the south, which they called the "Southern Land". But no one knew its size or shape, or whether it really existed.

Dutch sailors had sighted a large land, which they called New Guinea, because they found gold in its mountains. There were also pearl-oysters in the waters that washed its shores. Then they went farther south and reached a mainland. This is now called Australia, but the Dutch sailors called it New Holland. Its coast seemed uninviting, so they did not stop to explore it. In fact, they thought it might be joined to New Guinea. All these discoveries made Van Diemen anxious to send out more expeditions.

By this time people had learned more about exploring and seamanship. In the earlier expeditions

The multitude of islands in the Pacific Ocean

1" = 1500 MILES

sent out by the Spanish and Portuguese, many lives
had been lost through shipwreck, lack of food, mutiny,
and quarrels with natives. Van Diemen thought this
was not necessary. He chose to lead his expedition an
experienced sea captain, Abel Tasman, who was a
very cautious and careful commander. He gave
Tasman a pilot who, in all matters of navigation, was
to have equal authority with him. In case they dis-
agreed, there was to be a Council of Officers, which
was to have the last word.

Van Diemen called Tasman to his office in Batavia,
the capital of the Dutch East Indies. "Sail southward
until you come to New Holland," he said. "Then go
east and north again. If you find any unknown islands,
land on them, treat the natives kindly, and ask them
what goods they have for trade—especially gold and
silver."

"And, Captain—," the Governor's eyes twinkled,
"don't show any eagerness for these precious metals!
Pretend you don't know their value, and offer them
pieces of lead in exchange."

Captain Tasman left Batavia on the 14th of August
1642, with two ships and 110 men. His greatest
problem was, if he did find any new lands, how to
show on a map exactly where they were. The Pacific
Ocean was full of islands. Explorers kept sighting
them, and losing them again. The only way to find
these islands was by marking them on a good map.

The first good maps were made by geographers
after they had learned that the world was round.
They drew their maps on globes. To make their maps
accurate, they first drew lines on these globes, at equal
distances from one another. The lines were the kind
you would draw on a big round cake, if you wanted to
divide it up into equal shares.

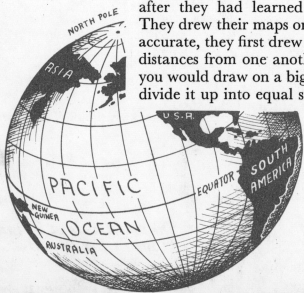

Some of the lines ran lengthways (that is, north and south). Others ran broadways (that is, east and west). The lines running lengthways on the globe were called "Lines of Longitude". The lines running broadways were called "Lines of Latitude". The distances between them were called "degrees".

To fix the position of any place on the globe, you take the nearest point at which two of these imaginary lines cross each other. The line of latitude shows how far north or south of the Equator the place is situated. The line of longtitude shows how far east or west of Greenwich (England) it is situated.

Most of the islands in the South Pacific Ocean lie south of the Equator. They are situated in southern latitudes. Also, most of them lie east of Greenwich. They are situated in eastern longitudes.

Batavia, from which Tasman started his voyage, is about eight degrees latitude south, and about 110 degrees longitude east.

Now in those days it was fairly easy for a sailor to fix the exact latitude of any spot, by observing the position of the sun and stars. But it was much more difficult to fix the longitude, because the only way to do this was by "time", measuring the hours and minutes of the day, east or west of Greenwich. Till after 1750, there was no exact instrument for measuring time. Clocks and watches were only roughly accurate. Chronometers, measuring "the split second", had not yet been invented.

Tasman therefore had to use a rougher method. He kept a record of how far he thought his ship had sailed each day, and in what direction. His ship's compass showed him the direction. His ship's "log" showed him the speed he sailed at.

Chronometer

A ship in distress sends a message for help and tells where it is by giving its latitude and longitude. Such a ship is on the map below at latitude 5 degrees S. and 130 degrees longitude E. See if you can locate it.

Lines of Longitude

140°   145°   150°

5°

Equator → 0°

NORTH ↑ ↓ SOUTH

5°

Lines of Latitude — 10°

15°

115°   120°   125°   130°   135°   140°   145°   150°

The "log" is a piece of wood tied to a rope with knots in it, spaced out equally along the rope. This log is thrown overboard to float behind the ship. As the rope is let out, a sailor counts the number of knots that go over the ship's stern in, say, one minute. This tells how far the ship has sailed in that time. The captain can then record how many "knots" the ship sails in an hour, or a whole day. The book in which the captain records this is called the ship's log-book, or (for short) the "log".

Tasman kept a "log" on his ship, and drew careful charts of the course of the vessel. He made maps of the places he explored, showing the latitude and longitude of each island, the height of the land, and the depth of the sea close to its shores.

All these records he took home with him, and gave to the Dutch Government. They were useful to the navigators who came after him. These navigators also brought home records, which added to their country's knowledge. The Dutch sailors found that, the more geography they knew, the more successful were their trading expeditions.

Modern instruments for measuring the speed of ships are now used instead of the simple method of knotted rope and log.

After leaving Batavia, Tasman sailed south and west of New Holland, then turned his ships eastward. On the 24th of November, he sighted land lying off the south coast of New Holland. He named it "Van Diemen's Land" after the Governor. Tasman did not know this was an island. He landed there, but was frightened by hearing trumpet-like noises in the trees, and seeing marks, which he took to be the tracks of great, wild beasts. He set up a post, carved his name on it, and then sailed away. This island is now called Tasmania. It is a province of Australia, and famous for its wool and apples.

A month later, Tasman again sighted land, this time a high, mountainous country which he named New Zealand, after a province in his own country. New Zealand turned out to be two islands, and Tasman sailed between them and anchored in a bay on the shores of the southern island. There he met a party of natives. They were Maoris—tall, strong, dark-skinned people, with hoarse voices and long black hair, combed in a knot on top of their heads. They decorated their bodies by scratching the skin and rubbing colour into the cuts. This is called "tattooing".

A tattooed Maori Chief

The Dutch began trading with the Maoris, and found them very intelligent. One day, however, the natives attacked a boatload of unarmed sailors and killed three of them. Without taking revenge, Tasman named the spot "Bay of Murderers", and sailed away.

From New Zealand, he struck out northward across the open sea, until he came to a group of small islands, now known as the Tonga, or Friendly Islands. The soil here was fertile, and the natives, who were like the Maoris, raised bananas and coconut palms. The dried meat of the coconuts was called *copra*, and supplied these natives with nourishing food. Another tree, the bread-fruit, looked much like the mulberry. The natives roasted the unripe berries, which were full of starch, and made a sort of bread.

Exploring these islands of the Pacific Ocean called for steady nerves and plenty of courage. The natives had strange customs. Some of them were cannibals, and ate their enemies. The islands were usually surrounded with coral reefs that were dangerous to ships. The waters were full of sharks. Hurricanes and earthquakes were frequent.

At the beginning of February, Tasman found
another group of islands, to which he gave Dutch
names, such as Amsterdam Island and Rotterdam
Island. Nowadays they are known as the Fiji
Archipelago.

Tasman landed on one of these islands, and found
the place "a perfect paradise", with long thick grass,
forests of mangrove and sandalwood and palms. The
natives seemed friendly, but Tasman did not stay long,
or explore the island fully. Something (we are not
sure what) upset him. Perhaps he had grown tired of
the constant danger of shipwreck, for every new island
meant new currents, reefs, shoals, and other dangers
to be avoided. At any rate, he called together his
Council and asked, "Shall we go on, or turn back?"

"There are too many fierce storms and strong
north-east winds in these parts," said the pilot. "If
we are not careful, they will blow our ships on the
coast of New Guinea, and then we shall be all
drowned. I vote to sail north and then run westward
for home."

When they reached Batavia, Van Diemen and the
officials of the East India Company were disappointed
by what they reported. They thought Tasman must
have been too timid, because he had brought back no
gold or silver.

But Tasman's caution had served his country well.
He had not brought back a rich cargo, but he had
brought his two ships and men home safely. He had
proved that Australia (New Holland) was an island.
And he had a wonderful set of charts of the Pacific
Ocean and its islands, as well as a *Journal* containing
his observations. Because of these charts, and because
he had treated the natives kindly, Tasman made the
way less dangerous for explorers who came after him.

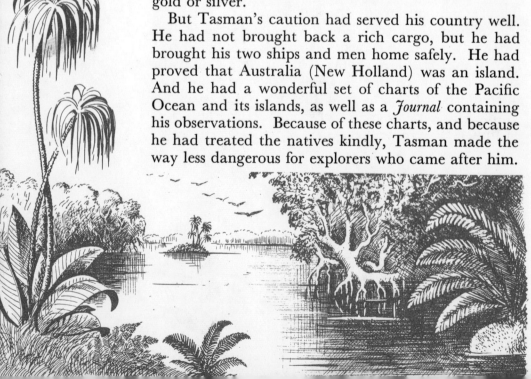

CAPTAIN COOK

WHEN Queen Elizabeth II was a guest of Queen Salote of Tonga, she went for a stroll in the royal palace grounds one morning. There she was shown a large tortoise.

"This tortoise is the oldest citizen of Tonga," someone told her Majesty. "Two hundred years ago he was given to the King of Tonga by Captain James Cook, when he visited this island. Our King honoured the tortoise by making him a chieftain of Tonga."

Here is the story of Captain James Cook, the explorer.

Columbus, da Gama, and Magellan are often called "explorers", but it would be truer to call them "traders". They went exploring to get gold and silver and spices from the natives of the lands they discovered, and to persuade them to become Christians. At the same time, they seemed to see no harm in plundering the new lands, and ill-treating the natives.

James Cook lived about 250 years later, when some of the peoples' ideas were changing. They still thought trade was important, but they wanted also to know all there was to know about new lands, new plants and animals, new climates, new races of men, even if this new knowledge was not going to make anyone richer.

In England, the Royal Society had been formed to encourage scientific enquiry. In 1769 its members decided to send out an expedition to Tahiti, one of the South Pacific islands, to make observations of the planets.

There are nine planets (or heavenly bodies) in the

The koala bear is a charming, harmless little animal which eats only the leaves of the eucalyptus tree. It is only found in Australia, and is there protected by law.

81

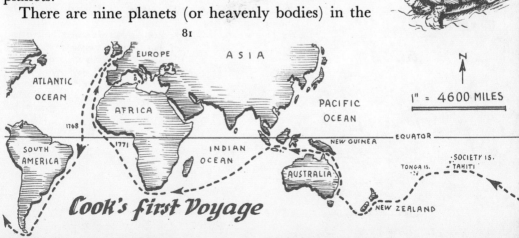

I" = 4600 MILES

Cook's first Voyage

Saturn

887.1 MILLIONS
OF MILES

Jupiter

483.91
MILLIONS OF MILES

Mars

Earth

Venus

Mercury

36.00 MILLIONS
OF MILES

67.28 MILLIONS
OF MILES

93.00 MILLIONS
OF MILES

Sun

141.71
MILLIONS OF MILES

sky, all moving in regular order around the sun. At certain times, some of these planets can be seen from the earth, passing between the earth and the sun. In 1769 the planet Venus was due to cross the face of the sun in this way. The English scientists wanted to observe this, and agreed that, for various reasons, they could get the best view, in the Southern Hemisphere, from the island of Tahiti.

To take the scientists there, the British Admiralty agreed to supply a ship, the *Endeavour*. Lieutenant Cook was chosen to command her.

As a boy, Cook had gone to sea in a ship carrying coal to Baltic ports. Then he joined the Royal Navy, and was made an officer, on account of his special skill in making charts. He made a survey of the currents and depths of the St. Lawrence River for General Wolfe, at the time of the taking of Quebec. Afterward he surveyed the coast of Newfoundland. He was forty years of age when he was given his great chance to become an explorer.

"You are to make friends with the natives of Tahiti," the Admiralty instructed him, "and draw up plans and descriptions of the islands. Then, as soon as the scientists have finished their work, you are to sail on southward, to see if there is any large mainland, or continent, in the South Pacific Ocean."

Most people at this time believed that there *was* such a continent, stretching all the way from the tip of South America to the tip of South Africa.

"If you find none," the instructions went on, "sail westward till you touch New Zealand, the land discovered by Tasman. Explore the coasts of this land, examine its soil and products, and, without running

Notice Venus on this drawing. The passing of this planet between the earth and the sun is called a TRANSIT of Venus. Drawings of heavenly bodies in a book cannot show sizes and distances as they should be.

into danger, make friends with the natives. Then visit Australia. All the time you are away, be sure to look after your crew's health, and keep your ship safe."

Lieutenant Cook mulled over his instructions. It was a great responsibility to take a ship with 72 officers and crew, 12 marines and the 11 passengers on board right around the globe, on a peaceful, scientific mission! And, as if that were not difficult enough, he must keep them all healthy and safe!

The British Admiralty had given Cook such a large crew because it expected that over one-half of them would die of scurvy, shipwreck, and other sea-perils during the voyage. Cook determined to avoid such heavy loss of life.

"There shall be strict health rules on the *Endeavour*," he ordered. "The ship must be kept spotlessly clean and well aired. Everyone on board is to be supplied with plenty of water. The crew are to be served fresh food and vegetables, and issued daily doses of lemon juice when we get to the tropics. This will check scurvy."

To reach Tahiti, the *Endeavour* sailed around Cape Horn, then steered north-west across the Pacific. The ship was 127 days at sea before coming to anchor in Matavai Bay, Tahiti. Tahiti was one of a group called by Cook the "Society Islands", after the Royal Society. It was a land of mountains and tropical forests, where the climate was warm, the scenery beautiful.

Like the natives of the Tonga Islands, the Tahitians (people of Tahiti) made bread from the bread-fruit tree. The milky juice of this tree they used to seal their dug-out canoes and make them water-proof. From the bark they made cloth, by first soaking it in

How a small body (such as the moon) can blot out the light of a big body (the sun) is easily shown by holding a pencil out in front of your face and closing one eye. Note that the pencil will shut out from your vision even a large tree, a few hundred feet away.

The moon is about ¼ the size of the earth and only 240,000 miles away.
Just as the earth moves around the sun, so the moon moves around the earth, taking 29½ days to do so. When it passes between the sun and the earth, the blocking of the sun's light from an observer on the earth is called a TOTAL ECLIPSE, if all the light is obstructed, and a PARTIAL ECLIPSE, if only part is cut off.

water and then pounding it with wooden clubs.

As the Tahitians had all they wanted, they were carefree and trusting. But, of course, they knew nothing of our ideas of right and wrong. For instance, stealing was not a crime in their eyes.

When the natives stole valuable tools from his ship, Cook had to think what to do. In such cases, he kept his head, never showed anger, but firmly corrected the offender. By his patience and wisdom he gained the respect of the Tahitians.

When the scientists had finished making their observations, Cook sailed the *Endeavour* southward to carry out the second part of his instructions. But now he met strong head winds and great ocean swells, which convinced him that no land lay in this direction. So he changed his course to the west, and in about a month reached the east coast of New Zealand.

An enormous dug-out Maori canoe, with 29 paddlers and a leader who stands in the centre. Planks were fastened along the sides to increase their height.

Here he found the natives were very different from the gentle Tahitians, although they belonged to the same race. For the first few days Cook had trouble with these Maoris (as they were called), who attacked the white men with long spears, heavy clubs and sling shots, and tried to steal their coats and weapons. To prove to the natives that he meant them no harm, Cook captured three young Maori warriors, treated them kindly, and sent them back with presents to their own people.

It was well that peace was restored in this way, for when the *Endeavour* began charting the coast of New Zealand, she soon met several large Maori war-canoes, which were bigger and faster than she was and carried more men! But the first Maoris had passed the word of friendship along the coast and wherever the *Endeavour* touched land, her reception was friendly.

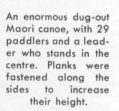

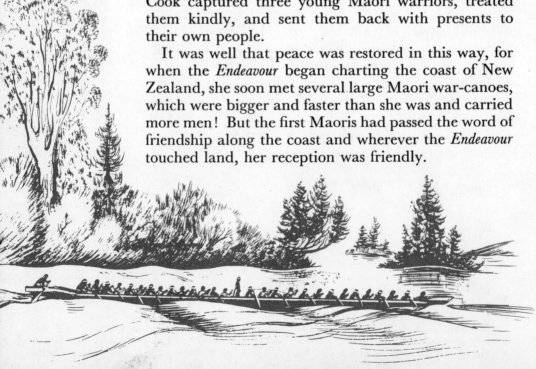

The Maoris were not only bolder, but cleverer than Tahitians. They invited Cook to visit them in their large huts, made of wood and dry grass. They wore clothing woven out of strips of leaves, tattooed their faces in red and black, and ornamented their noses and ears with pieces of bone and feathers. They had sharp axes and chisels, made of stone.

After sailing right around the two main islands of New Zealand, and exploring Cook Strait that divides them, the *Endeavour* continued her voyage to the east coast of Australia. Cook was the first white man to land on Australian soil, at Botany Bay, where today the modern city of Sydney stands. Botany Bay got its name from the number of plants and trees found there by the scientists of Cook's expedition. Among these trees was the gum, or eucalyptus, which has thick, evergreen leaves with a spicy smell.

At Botany Bay Cook met the natives, or aborigines, of Australia. They were more difficult to deal with than the people of Tahiti or New Zealand. The aborigines did not want to trade, because they had no use for white men's goods. They were a wandering people, who built no homes, but sheltered in tree branches. They dressed in the skins of the animals they hunted, and ate whatever food they could find in the bush (or scrub) and water, such as grubs, roots, seeds, turtles, and fish. Their best weapon was the boomerang, a curved stick that returned through the air to its thrower, if it missed its mark.

An Australian Aborigine with spear and boomerang

Cook sailed north along the east coast of Australia, inside the beautiful, but dangerous, line of coral reefs known as the Great Barrier Reef. The line is more than 1,000 miles long, and coloured (pink, blue, mauve, and green) from the bodies of the corals—tiny sea-animals—from which the reefs are made.

Peculiar Coral forms on the Great Barrier Reef

Cook took possession of the east coast of Australia for England. Then sailing north and west, he made the discovery that New Guinea was an island, separated from Australia by a sea-way through which the *Endeavour* sailed. Before this, navigators had supposed New Guinea was part of the mainland. Continuing his course westward along the south coast of Java, Cook reached Batavia, where he stopped to repair his ship. Here, on account of the unhealthy climate, some of his men caught tropical fever and died.

On the 13th of July 1771 Cook landed in England, after having been away three years. He brought home in good health fifty-six of those who had originally sailed with him. The ship's goat also made the trip in safety. She was, as far as we know, the first animal to travel around the world!

Cook was not allowed to enjoy home life for long. The Government promoted him to the rank of captain, and asked him to lead a second expedition to the South Seas. This time he was to find out, once for all, whether there was or was not a large continent lying to the south of Australia and New Zealand.

Eucalyptus Tree and flower

Cook sailed from England in 1772 with two ships, the *Resolution* and the *Adventure*, and was away for three full years! He first touched at Cape Town in South Africa to take plenty of fresh water and food on board. Then he steered boldly south into the icy waters of the Antarctic. He planned to sail eastward, keeping a sharp lookout for land.

1" = 4600 MILES

The ships were beset with icebergs, frozen seas, and fogs, and soon became separated from one another. The *Resolution*, in which Cook sailed, continued cruising in the Antarctic for over 100 days, covering 3,500 miles without sighting land. Cook then turned north-

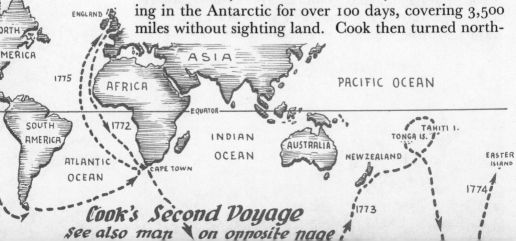

Cook's Second Voyage
see also map on opposite page

ward to New Zealand, where he found the *Adventure*, safe and sound.

Both ships sailed on to Tahiti, and from there visited the Tonga Islands, where the visitors were shown a pool in which Tasman had bathed 200 years earlier. Cook left some pigs for the Islanders, thinking they would do well there. To this day, there is a breed of Tonga pigs called "Captain Cookers"!

Cook had such a good impression of the natives of these islands that he named them the "Friendly Islands". Certainly Queen Salote of Tonga (one of the Friendly Islands) was one of the friendliest and most popular visitors attending the Coronation of Queen Elizabeth II in London in 1953.

Now the *Resolution*, alone, turned southward to penetrate the Antarctic again. The cold was so intense that the ship's rigging became like metal wires and the sails froze so hard they could not be handled! Still there was no sign of any land, only islands of floating ice. In January 1774, the ship reached a solid wall of ice and was forced to turn back.

On the homeward voyage, by way of the Cape of Good Hope, several groups of islands were discovered in the Pacific. One was Easter Island, where stand twenty-seven large black statues, carved and set up by some unknown people of the past.

When he reached England, Cook was presented to the King and promoted again. Then he was asked to take charge of a third expedition.

This time the British Government wanted him to help solve the secret of the North-West Passage, from Europe to Asia, by way of North America. For over 200 years this secret had baffled explorers, many of whom had lost their lives in its search. Now the British Admiralty planned to send out one expedition

Statues on Easter Island

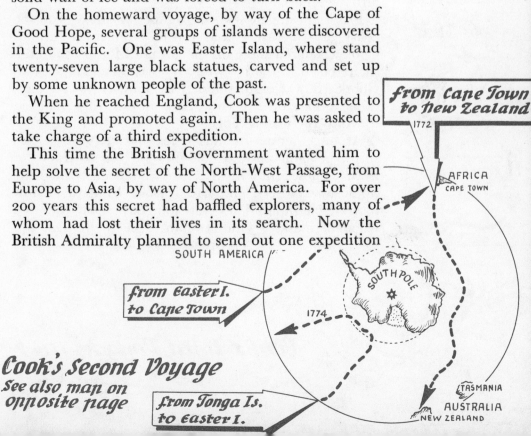

from Cape Town to New Zealand
1772

AFRICA
CAPE TOWN

SOUTH AMERICA

from Easter I. to Cape Town

SOUTH POLE

1774

Cook's Second Voyage
See also map on opposite page

from Tonga Is. to Easter I.

TASMANIA
AUSTRALIA
NEW ZEALAND

to sail north-west from the Atlantic, and another to sail north-east from the Pacific.

Cook was chosen to lead the expedition from the Pacific. He set out in the summer of 1776 with two ships, the *Resolution* and the *Discovery*. All earlier explorers who had sailed around the globe had done so by going west. Cook was instructed to proceed in the opposite direction, sailing first around Africa, then north-east through the Pacific to the west coast of North America.

On the way, Cook revisited Tasmania, New Zealand, and Tahiti. He had brought a new marvel to show his friends, the Tahitians—a horse! He rode all around the island on it, to show them what a fine, useful animal this was!

After this, he visited the Hawaiian Islands, in the centre of the Pacific Ocean. The people of Hawaii were like the Tahitians, except that they had learned what iron was, and asked Cook to trade some pieces of this metal for head-dresses which they wove from birds' feathers.

From Hawaii the two ships sailed north-west to the coast of California, and on to Vancouver Island. Cook anchored there on the 30th of March 1778, in a sheltered bay on its western coast, called Nootka. Nootka Bay was surrounded by snow-capped mountains, and clothed with thick forests that reached down to the water's edge.

At once many Indians came out to visit Cook's ships, bringing furs, which they offered to trade for iron. These Indians had already been visited by Spanish explorers, and had learned from them how to drive bargains. They were fond of wearing coloured wooden masks. One Indian decked himself out

ATLANTIC
OCEAN

ICELAND

ENGLAND

EUROPE

AFRICA

EQUATOR

1776

INDIAN
OCEAN

Cook's third Voyage 1776-9

CAPE TOWN

N

1" = 1800 MILES

proudly in a kettle, which he had bought from the white men for a mask!

Cook visited the houses of these Indians, and saw the carved totem poles that they had set up in front of them.

The summer of 1778 was given up to the search for the North-West Passage. Cook's ships followed the North American coastline northward as far as Una-laska, at the south-western top of Alaska. The natives here had an Asiatic appearance, and traded with Russians who had followed after Bering's explorations.

From Alaska, Cook crossed Bering Sea to St. Lawrence Bay on the mainland of Asia. Pushing on north, he noticed that the American and Asian coasts curved away to the north-east and north-west, showing that he was entering the Polar Sea. Then he sighted Icy Cape, the northermost point of the American continent, and found his way barred by heavy pack ice, on which sat herds of walrus. These provided a welcome supply of fresh meat for his men.

Cook's ships now needed repairs, so he turned south again. He had not found the North-West Passage. But at Unalaska he met Russian traders, who promised to send his precious maps and charts back to England through Russia, which they did.

In January 1779, Cook reached Hawaii on his return journey. He found that all sorts of amazing stories had spread about among the natives.

"The White Men are volcanoes, that spit fire and smoke (tobacco) from their mouths! They have side doors (pockets) in their bodies! Their bodies are full of treasures. Cook himself is a god!"

The Hawaiians received Cook with great reverence, and supplied his ships with food and water. But

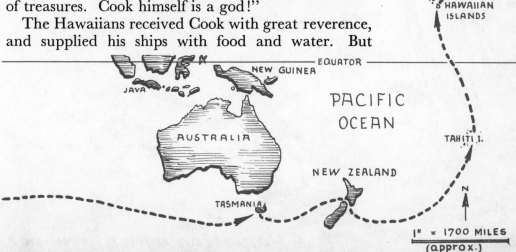

later, a native stole a tool from an English sailor. When Cook landed, and tried to set the matter right, he was attacked and stabbed to death by the natives. His officers continued the voyage, and brought the two ships safely home to England.

When Cook's *Journals* were published, everyone realized that Britain had lost one of her greatest explorers. He had sailed over 50,000 miles, and gone around the world twice on peaceful journeys. By paying attention to health rules, he had kept his crews free of scurvy, and proved that it was possible to explore without heavy loss of life.

Perhaps sometime you will be in London, England, and see his statue and read the inscription at its base:

Circumnavigator of the Globe—Explorer of the Pacific Ocean—He laid the foundations of the British Empire in Australia and New Zealand—He charted the shores of Newfoundland and traversed the Ocean Gates of Canada both East and West.

In Cook's time, it took at least two years to sail around the world. Today, if you are in a hurry, you can fly around it in a few days.

Queen Elizabeth II, on her world tour in 1953 and 1954, spent six months visiting each part of the British Commonwealth. In the Pacific she sailed along the same routes as Cook, and visited many of the places he had discovered. The people who lived there received her with enthusiasm and expressions of love and loyalty. Perhaps this was partly because, 200 years before, Captain Cook had treated the natives so well, and had helped to improve their lives by bringing them new plants and animals, and new ideas. His voyages of exploration made the world seem a smaller and friendlier place than it had been before.

A Hawaiian with a throw-net

BERING

TASMAN, the Dutch navigator, had proved that careful explorers could bring their ships and crews home safely, without shipwreck or serious trouble with the natives. But sometimes explorers were set tasks so dangerous they lost their lives in carrying them out.

One of these unlucky ones was Vitus Bering, a Danish sailor, who took service in the navy of Peter the Great, the Tsar (or King) of Russia.

Peter, an able but cruel ruler, made Russia united and powerful for the first time in her history. Before this, Russia had been invaded by Mongols from Asia, who destroyed her cities and made her people poor and backward. When Peter came to the throne, he encouraged visitors from Western Europe to enter Russia. They said his people were no better than savages.

Peter decided to travel abroad and see for himself what these western countries were like, in order that he could learn how to improve the condition of his own country. He visited France and England, where he saw ships being built. He met seamen who had sailed on voyages of exploration and discovered new lands. Peter decided the Russians must do the same.

But how? Most of the coastline of Russia faced the Arctic Ocean, where ships could not sail because of the ice. If there were to be voyages of exploration, they would have to start on the far east coast of Russia, where the sea was free of ice.

Some of Peter's subjects had been so cruelly treated that they had left their homes and moved eastward. These people, called *Cossacks*, wandered across Siberia, the northern half of Asia, making small settlements.

91

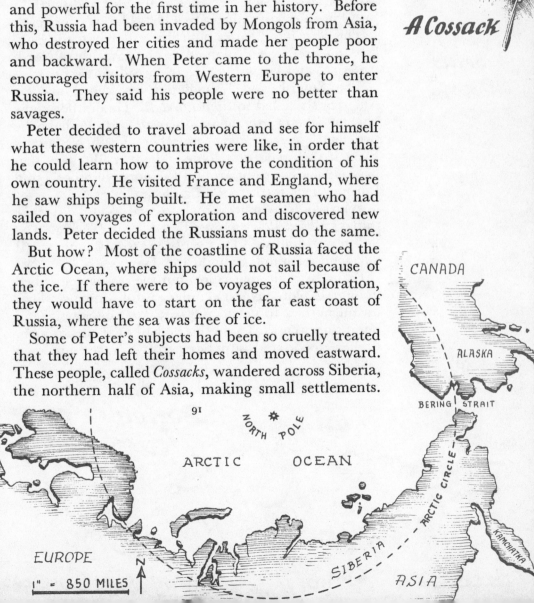

A Cossack

One day Tsar Peter called the leaders of the Cossacks back to Moscow. "What is Siberia like?" he asked.

"Little Father," they answered, using the familiar name that all Russians gave to their Tsar, "the country is rich in furs and fish, but full of great rivers and lakes which are hard to cross. Also, it is bitterly cold, and life is very hard there."

"Ah," said the Tsar. "What lies north of Siberia?"

"A great frozen sea, Little Father."

"And where does Siberia end?"

"Little Father, that we do not know. The natives, called *Chukchi*, say it stretches to the east and north."

"Oho—perhaps Siberia reaches as far as America!"

The Tsar had heard about the settlements the English and French had planted on the east side of North America, and knew these were spreading westward.

Seals

The English and French did not know how far America stretched to the *north-west*. He did not know how far Siberia stretched to the *north-east*. Perhaps the two lands were joined, somewhere north of Japan? Even if they were not joined, there might be a sea-passage leading right around the north of Siberia and Europe, back to the Atlantic Ocean.

Who would be a good man to send to find out these things? Tsar Peter remembered Vitus Bering, who had served him well for twenty years in the navy. "I will send for him," thought the Tsar.

Bering was an able sailor, but the sea he was called upon to explore lay 3,000 miles east of Moscow. That meant he had to get to the east coast of Siberia and build ships there. To do this he had to transport men, timber, food, and supplies across a vast, unknown

DENMARK

Bering's first

ARCTIC

ARCTIC CIRCLE

OB RIVER

N

1" = 640 MILES

MOSCOW

wilderness, frozen for a good part of the year.

Siberia is about as large as Canada, and has the same climate. In Bering's time, Russia had no railways, or other means of rapid travel. Everything had to be pulled in carts or sleds, by horses or by hand, or floated on rafts.

Hardly had Bering started on his task, when Tsar Peter died. But Bering was a determined man, and went on carrying out orders. After three years of terrible toil, he had everything ready at a small seaport called Okhotsk on the east coast of Siberia, north of Japan. He had built a small ship, the *St. Gabriel*, and loaded her with provisions for one year. Two assistants, Spanberg, a Dane, and Chirikov, a Russian, were to accompany him on this voyage.

The *St. Gabriel* had first to sail around Kamchatka, the long peninsula that juts out from North-East Siberia in the direction of Japan. Then Bering could follow the Siberian coastline northward.

In August 1728, he found himself in the Bay of Anadyr, far up the Siberian coast and nearly at the Arctic Circle. At this time of year the weather was very bad for sailing. There was much fog and drizzle, broken by sudden squalls of wind.

Bering wanted to question the Chukchi who dressed in skins and looked like the Eskimos of Northern Canada. But the Chukchi seemed afraid of the Russians. Bering had difficulty in making them understand what he wanted. At last one Chukchi, braver than the rest, made himself a pair of water-wings out of fish-bladders, and swam out to the *St. Gabriel*.

"What is the shape of the land to the north of here?" Bering asked him.

"First you will pass two big bays," came the

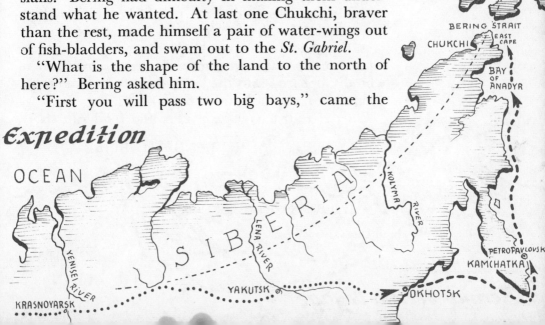

Expedition

OCEAN

ALASKA

BERING STRAIT
EAST CAPE
CHUKCHI
BAY OF ANADYR

SIBERIA

KOLYMA RIVER

LENA RIVER

YENSEI RIVER

KRASNOYARSK

YAKUTSK

OKHOTSK

PETROPAVLOVSK
KAMCHATKA

A Polar Bear

answer. "Then the land turns westward as far as the Kolyma River, where we go to hunt for reindeer."

Bering sailed north to East Cape, where he could see for himself that the land turned westward. He was inside the narrow passage, later called after him, *Bering Strait*. If the weather had not been foggy, he could have seen across this strait to Alaska, in North America.

Chirikov wanted Bering to continue his voyage farther north and west, to the Kolyma River. But Spanberg warned him it was too late in the year to attempt this. Bering chose safety first, and brought the *St. Gabriel* back to Okhotsk.

Then Bering made a journey to Moscow to report to the Empress Anna, who now sat on the throne of Russia. She was disappointed that he had not gone farther. He must try again, she ordered.

More heartbreaking preparations had now to be made. To make matters worse, the Empress did not give Bering enough money to buy the things he needed for the voyage. Instead, she sent a man to help him who was a bungler and gave Bering endless trouble.

This time the preparations took Bering seven years, but at last he had two ships, the *St. Peter* and the *St. Paul*, provisioned and manned with 76 men each.

Bering commanded the *St. Peter*, and took with him a young German scientist, George Steller, to act as ship's doctor and to study any plants and animals they might find. Chirikov commanded the *St. Paul*. They sailed in June 1740, from the port of Petropavlovsk on Kamchatka, for the west coast of North America.

A heavy fog soon parted the two ships. Chirikov landed on an unknown shore. He lost fourteen men, who disappeared into the bush and never came back. Then in a panic he headed for home.

On the return voyage, water and food ran short,

SIBERIA

Bering's Second Voyage

scurvy broke out, and the *St. Paul* crept back to Petropavlovsk with only fifty-five men. Chirikov himself developed tuberculosis on the voyage, and never recovered from this illness.

The fate of Bering and the *St. Peter* was even worse. After a long, vain search for the *St. Paul*, Bering pushed on alone across the North Pacific Ocean. After several days, he saw sea-otters swimming near his ship, and knew that he was coming to land. He anchored off a shining sandy beach, back of which stretched the mountains and thick evergreen forests of Alaska.

A Sea Otter

"This is America!" cried Steller. "Let us land and explore the country!"

For a moment, hope and joy filled the hearts of the Russians. But Bering himself showed no pleasure. He was suffering from scurvy, and worn out by fifteen years of trouble he had been through.

"Yes, we will land," agreed Bering, "but only for one day, to take fresh water on board. If we stay here longer, winter will set in, and then we shall starve."

Steller spent his one day ashore in a feverish search. He found the bones of animals, picked specimens of flowers and plants, and gathered together a few tools and weapons from a deserted Indian camp. With the aid of these materials, he was able to write a book.

The *St. Peter* started on her homeward journey, but ran into winds, blinding rainstorms, and thick fogs. Bering had expected to reach Kamchatka in four days, but the crossing took forty! Every day some member of the crew died of cold, hunger, or scurvy. When they were in sight of Kamchatka, the ship was wrecked and they were forced to land on a deserted island.

Here they built a rough hut of stones and earth, and

Coastline of Alaska

succeeded in killing enough game to keep them alive. They stayed on the island a year, without being rescued. In the dark days of mid-winter, Vitus Bering died of scurvy.

Then Steller took charge and organized the remaining men into three teams, to get wood, water, and food. When summer came, they took broken timbers from the *St. Peter* and built a boat, forty-two feet long. Into this frail craft Steller crowded the forty-five men who were left, with all their gear and food.

Luckily the weather held good. After two weeks they reached Petropavlovsk, where they were welcomed as men risen from the dead. Steller was so weakened from the voyages that he did not survive long.

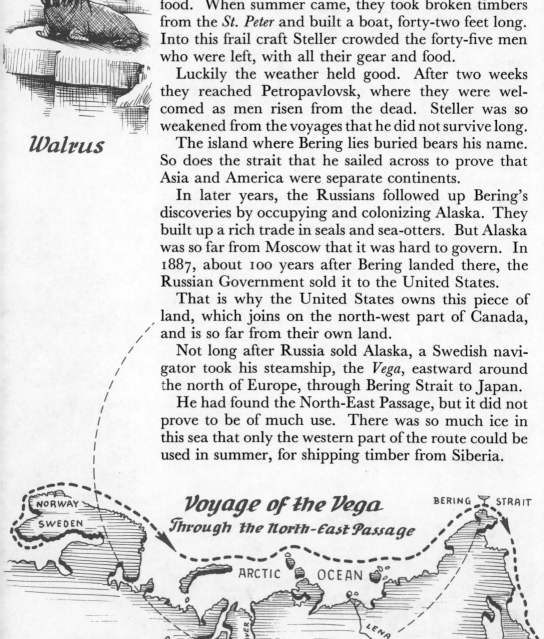

Walrus

The island where Bering lies buried bears his name. So does the strait that he sailed across to prove that Asia and America were separate continents.

In later years, the Russians followed up Bering's discoveries by occupying and colonizing Alaska. They built up a rich trade in seals and sea-otters. But Alaska was so far from Moscow that it was hard to govern. In 1887, about 100 years after Bering landed there, the Russian Government sold it to the United States.

That is why the United States owns this piece of land, which joins on the north-west part of Canada, and is so far from their own land.

Not long after Russia sold Alaska, a Swedish navigator took his steamship, the *Vega*, eastward around the north of Europe, through Bering Strait to Japan.

He had found the North-East Passage, but it did not prove to be of much use. There was so much ice in this sea that only the western part of the route could be used in summer, for shipping timber from Siberia.

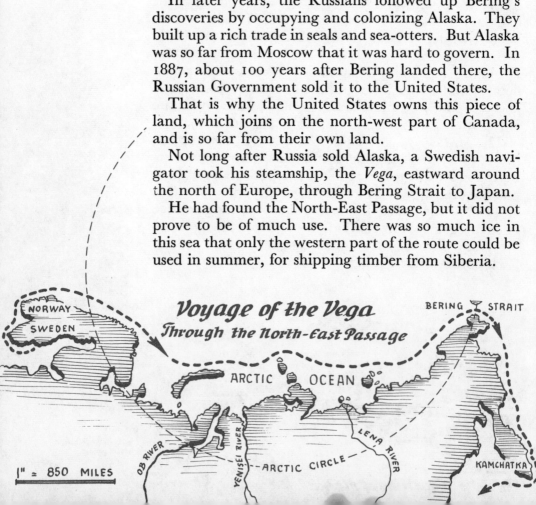

Voyage of the Vega
Through the North-East Passage

NORWAY
SWEDEN
BERING STRAIT
ARCTIC OCEAN
OB RIVER
YENISEI RIVER
ARCTIC CIRCLE
LENA RIVER
KAMCHATKA

1" ≈ 850 MILES

TO ASIA THROUGH POLAR SEAS

THE SEARCH FOR THE NORTH-WEST PASSAGE

SEBASTIAN CABOT, after his second voyage, had brought home to England exciting news. He declared he had seen the entrance to a great sea-passage leading between Greenland and North America. This passage seemed to lead north-west. Perhaps it might lead right around the north coast of America, and so open a way for English ships to sail to India and China?

Many sailors thought they would like to try and find this North-West Passage. They were encouraged by reading a book written by two Italian brothers named Zeno. This told the story of a journey to the Far North, supposed to have been made by one of their ancestors. The journey was imaginary, but the Zenos persuaded a well known map-maker to draw a map for their book. This map was so well drawn, and looked so accurate, that for the next 200 years sailors thought it must be a reliable guide to the Far North.

The map was really quite wrong, because it showed the east coast of Greenland joined to the north coast of Norway, and several imaginary islands. It also showed a large, open sea-way in the north-west

corner, off Greenland. This was marked "Passage to
the Indies". Many people felt sure that this was the
same passage that Sebastian Cabot had seen.

Martin Frobisher

Martin Frobisher, a brave seaman who lived in the
days of Queen Elizabeth I, was the first to try and find
Cabot's passage. His hero was Magellan. He had
read the story of Magellan's voyage, and wanted to
sail around the world himself.

But he thought he would go by the northern, instead
of the southern route. By using the Zenos' map, he
hoped to reach the Pacific by sailing around the north
coast of North America.

"This passage," he said, "is the only thing in the
world that is yet undone. It is as evident as the
English Channel."

In 1576 a company that had been formed to pro-
mote trade with Russia gave Frobisher two ships to
explore with. Sailing north-west from England, he
sighted a land which, he said, looked like a mass of
church steeples crowned with snow. These were the
mountains and glaciers of Greenland. Frobisher, so
far as we know, was the first European to see them
since Viking days.

He pushed on westward and reached a large piece
of land lying off the north-east coast of America. This
was afterward called Baffin Island. Frobisher anchored in a bay which was later named, after him,
Frobisher Bay. Here he met Eskimos in *kayaks*. He
thought they must be Chinese, on account of their
round faces, flat noses, and slanting eyes. In fact,
these people *had* come to North America from Asia,
centuries ago, crossing from Siberia to Alaska by boat
in summer, or by sledge in winter.

Frobisher's first Voyage

Frobisher did not make friends with these Eskimos, and so missed a good chance to learn about life in the Far North. When he sailed home, he had little to show for his voyage, except an odd-looking piece of shiny black stone that he had picked up on the shore of the bay.

But this glistening stone excited much wonder in England. "It is a piece of ore containing gold!" people declared.

A Company was formed to mine these stones. Queen Elizabeth herself bought shares in this company. She gave the new land a Latin name "Meta Incognita", meaning in English "Worth Unknown". Frobisher was sent out on a second expedition and, after a skirmish with the Eskimos, returned home with 200 tons of this black ore.

Next it was decided to establish a fort and a colony at "Worth Unknown". Frobisher was sent out again with fifteen ships, 100 settlers, provisions, and even a ready-made wooden house for them to live in. But after visiting Greenland, the ships sailed on a westerly course and ran into gales, icebergs, fogs, and blizzards. These were caused by the cold currents from the Arctic Ocean which flow southward along the coast of Baffin Island.

Frobisher's ships were badly damaged by storms, and when the explorers landed at "Worth Unknown", they found that only two sides of the house they had brought with them were left. Also, they had not enough food to last through the winter. So they took on board another large cargo of ore, and sailed for home.

Here they were greeted with the unpleasant news that the black ore had been thoroughly analysed and

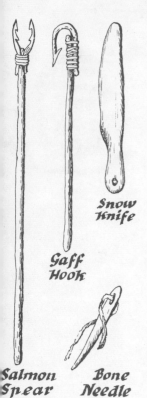

Snow Knife

Gaff Hook

Salmon Spear   *Bone Needle*

found to be worthless! The Company then went out of business, and Frobisher sailed on no more voyages of exploration. However, he helped to defeat the Spanish Armada in 1588, and Queen Elizabeth made him a knight, as a reward for his services.

Everyone forgot about the black ore, which was probably graphite. No one thought of looking for minerals in this land of ice and fog. The great iron beds of Labrador, south of the place where Frobisher landed, were not discovered for almost 300 years!

John Davis

However, the seamen of England did not forget about the North-West Passage. In 1584 the North-West Company was specially formed, to search for it. This Company chartered two ships, and put them in charge of John Davis, one of the best navigators of his time. Davis first explored the east and west coasts of Greenland, and landed near the present settlement of Godthaab.

He was much cleverer than Frobisher in dealing with the Eskimos. He had his ship's fiddlers strike up a tune, ordered his sailors to dance, and invited the Eskimos to join in. Soon they made friends with him and his men. Davis was careful to treat the Eskimos honestly. They, in turn, were honest with him. As a result, he learned a good deal about the climate, flowers, and animals of the Arctic. Especially, he learned how the Eskimos survived in this cold land, getting food by hunting reindeer, caribou, and seals, and making clothes and shelters out of the skins of these animals.

Next summer Davis set out again with four ships. He was now able to divide his fleet into two, and to

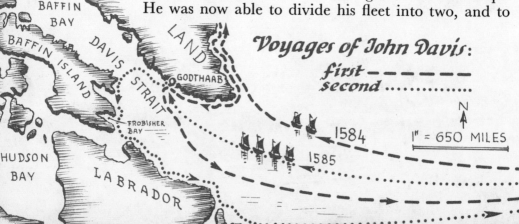

GREEN

BAFFIN BAY

BAFFIN ISLAND

DAVIS STRAIT

LAND

GODTHAAB

FROBISHER BAY

HUDSON BAY

LABRADOR

Voyages of John Davis:
first ― ― ― ―
second ··············

1584

1585

N

1" = 650 MILES

explore both the east and the west coasts of Greenland at the same time. In his own ship he tried to sail north beyond Godthaab, but was forced back by a great mass of pack-ice.

So he crossed from Greenland to the mainland of North America, where he found Frobisher Bay, and afterward explored the coast of Labrador as far south as Newfoundland. When Davis returned to England he reported that there was so much fish off the Newfoundland coast that the catches would pay for all future voyages of exploration in these parts!

On his third expedition, Davis sent two ships to fish off Newfoundland, while he himself sailed north again from Godthaab. His ship sprang a leak, but he pushed on to a headland on the Greenland coast beyond Latitude 72 degrees. This was the farthest north reached by any sailor up to this date.

From there winds drove him westward till he ran into a great line of broken ice-floes. This ice was eight feet thick and extended for 200 miles. But the ice-floes did not remain in one place. They slowly drifted southward, carried by sea currents. Davis's ship drifted with the ice, past the coast of "Meta Incognita", which he did not recognize because it was too far off. At last the ice began to break up, and he reached the mouth of a strait which led westward.

Davis would have liked to explore this strait, but dared not. The tide rushed in and out of it at a great speed, causing the water at high tide to rise to a height of thirty or forty feet above the level of the ocean at its mouth. Davis thought this rising tide looked like great rapids, or, as he called it, "a mighty overfall, with circular motions like whirlpools".

The strait, which Davis discovered but did not

The explorers must have had splendid views of the Northern Lights which take many different shapes. Those shown here are like curtains. It is thought that these lights are caused by particles thrown off by the sun. As they near the earth they are attracted toward the Magnetic North Pole.

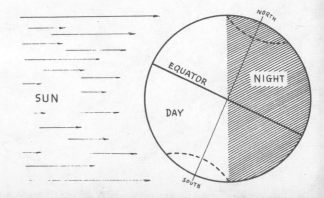

This diagram shows why there is continuous night above the Arctic Circle when the North Pole is tilted away from the sun.

SUN

NORTH

EQUATOR

NIGHT

DAY

SOUTH

sun ray
sight box

line of
sight to horizon

Davis's Quadrant

Because of ocean currents and storms, ships may get off course in the wide ocean out of sight of land. Sometimes they are in danger of running aground on reefs or shoals, as Drake did (page 72). By fixing their location with an instrument such as Davis's quadrant they can alter their direction if necessary to avoid danger and to proceed to their destination.

80° GREENLAND

BAFFIN BAY

BAFFIN ISLAND

70°

DAVIS STRAIT

ARCTIC CIRCLE

GODTHAAB

HUDSON ST.

60°

The third Voyage of John Davis

ATLANTIC OCEAN

HUDSON BAY

LABRADOR

50°

NEWFOUNDLAND

enter, led direct into Hudson Bay.

Davis returned home the year before Spain sent her Armada, or great fleet, to conquer England. Englishmen were so busy planning how to meet this attack, that they could not think of sending men or ships on more voyages of exploration.

So Davis stayed at home writing an account of his voyages, to help future explorers. He also invented an instrument called a Davis Quadrant, which made it easier for sailors to fix their location by observing from the deck of the ship the angle the sun's rays made with the horizon at a certain time of day. By using ocean charts and tables worked out by scientists the sailors could then determine just where they were.

Before Davis's time other instruments had been employed for this purpose. Columbus used the sea-quadrant. There was also the cross-staff, which was invented later. All of these required the seaman to look directly at the sun, with risk of injury to his eye.

Davis's quadrant made it possible to measure the necessary angle with the observer's back to the sun. A sight attached to the upper scale was moved so that the image of the sun fell on the sight-box just at the point where the line from the observer's eye to the horizon passed through a tiny hole in it. A small mirror was also used to reflect the sun's image from the sight-box to the eye. Because the sight on the lower scale could also be moved, it was possible to measure the angle whether the sun were lower or higher in the heavens than shown in the illustration to the left.

Seamen were glad to have an instrument that saved their eyes, and Davis's quadrant was used even after the sextant was invented, about 100 years later.

Henry Hudson

It was twenty-five years after Davis's last expedition before the English took up the search for the North-West Passage again. Then a new company, the Merchant Adventurers, provided a ship for this purpose, called the *Discovery*. They gave command of it to Henry Hudson.

Captain Hudson had already made two voyages to the Arctic to explore Greenland and the Island of Spitzbergen. He had also explored the Hudson River on the east coast of North America for the Dutch.

Now the Merchant Adventurers asked him to find the strait that John Davis had seen, and to follow it through in the hope of reaching the Pacific Ocean. This was in 1610.

No doubt Captain Hudson expected a successful voyage and a safe return. There was enough food on board the *Discovery* for a six months' cruise. He took along with him his young son John to keep him company. But he was not wise in the selection of his crew. Most of them were rascals, especially a young good-for-nothing fellow named Henry Greene.

At first all went well. They reached Greenland, crossed Davis Strait, and found the entrance to the passage that Davis had described as a "mighty over-fall". They followed this strait through till it opened out into a wide expanse of water. This was Hudson Bay.

Probably Hudson thought he had reached the Pacific Ocean. He sailed southward along the east shore of the bay, until he came to James Bay. There the *Discovery* caught fast in the ice. She could go neither forward nor back. Winter was setting in. They had food enough left for only two months. Yet

Reindeer

The Voyage of Hudson

Ptarmigan

here they must stay for the next six months until the ice melted in the summer.

It was a dismal spot. The shores of James Bay were flat, and covered with hummocks of ice. The only plants were small Arctic willows, whose twigs barely showed above the snow. The only trees were small evergreens bent over and dwarfed by the cruel winds that blew across the bay.

Hudson organized hunting and fishing parties to keep his men active and add to their stock of food. They lived chiefly on ptarmigan and other wild fowl which they shot—also on Arctic moss, which they gathered. But the bitter cold and the long, dark winter nights made his men dispirited, and scurvy broke out among them.

The crew began to blame Hudson for their troubles. He had never been popular with his men, who accused him of unfair distribution of the food. Also he had quarrelled with his officers, and annoyed them by showing favours to worthless persons like Greene.

In June, the ice melted and the *Discovery* was free to sail again. The men supposed that Hudson would set sail for England. But he announced that he would restock his ship's food supply with sea-birds' eggs, and continue his search for the North-West Passage. The crew could not endure the thought of this.

At sunrise one day Captain Hudson was seized and bound as he came out of his cabin to go on deck. The few officers and men who remained loyal to him were also overpowered. Then the mutineers, headed by Greene, took charge of the ship.

One of the small, open boats was brought alongside the *Discovery*. Into it were forced four of the crew who were sick, three men who were loyal to Hudson, the

Captain himself, and his son John. They were given a musket, some powder and shot, some meal, and an iron pot. Then all nine were turned adrift, to meet a certain, but lingering death.

The thirteen mutineers now tried to take the *Discovery* back to England. Five, including Greene, were killed on the way, in a skirmish with Eskimos. The rest reached home, where they were put on trial for the murder of Hudson. However they were let go free, partly because the facts were difficult to prove, partly because experienced Arctic seamen were scarce. Their services were needed for a new voyage.

Arctic Terns

William Baffin

In 1616, the *Discovery* was sent out again, this time commanded by William Baffin. He was not only a skilful seaman, but a man of science. He had taught himself astronomy, and during all his voyages took exact observations and kept careful records. On this voyage, he was to sail farther north into the Arctic than any other explorer for the next 230 years!

Baffin had made up his mind to follow the course of Davis, who had sailed north until his way had been barred by pack-ice. Baffin hoped for better luck— perhaps he could steer past the ice and find open water beyond it!

He sailed up the west coast of Greenland till he came to the spot where Davis had turned back. Here huge ice-floes again blocked the way. But it was early in the year, and Baffin thought he would wait. Sure enough, as the summer advanced, the ice began to open up. The *Discovery* was able to edge its way forward slowly, twisting and turning through the sea of pack-ice. Sometimes, when they could not use their

ARCTIC OCEAN

N

I" = 850 MILES

CANADA

GREENLAND

LANCASTER SD.

BAFFIN BAY

DAVIS STRAIT

1616

BAFFIN ISLAND

HUDSON STRAIT

LABRADOR

HUDSON BAY

The Voyage of Baffin

sails, they lowered the ships' boats and used them to tug the *Discovery* along narrow channels of water between the ice-floes.

On the 1st of July, the ship reached a great expanse of sea, afterward called Baffin Bay. Still William Baffin pushed ahead, until he was 300 miles north of the spot where Davis had turned back.

Before him now lay several large islands, black and flat. Between them were straits or "sounds". One of these sounds was afterward called Lancaster Sound, after Sir James Lancaster, a famous trader with the East India Company, who had encouraged Hudson to try and find a sea-way to India through the North-West Passage. Lancaster Sound was the gateway to this passage! But Baffin had no way of knowing this. With his crew badly crippled by scurvy, he turned back.

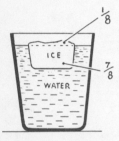

The danger of an iceberg to ships is greatly increased because ⅞th of it are under water and cannot be seen. It may thus have an invisible underwater projection extending hundreds of feet from the visible portion.

When he reached England, he told people of the great bay he had found north of the pack-ice, and described the sound leading to the West. But nobody would believe he had sailed this far north. His wonderful voyage seemed to have been made in vain.

It was 200 years before English seamen again took up the search for the North-West Passage. By that time English ships were bigger, and scientific knowledge was greater. Before further voyages were taken, Baffin's records were carefully studied. Navigators now believed that these were correct, and further expeditions were sent out, by way of Lancaster Sound.

FRANKLIN

DID you ever look at the places on a map and wonder how they got their names? Behind each name there is a story.

You will see at the far north of the map of North America such names as: Cabot Strait, Hudson Bay, Frobisher Bay, Davis Strait and Baffin Island. All these places were named in honour of explorers who went in search of the North-West Passage.

If you look more closely at this part of the map of North America, you will find a narrow passage called Franklin Strait. This was named after Sir John Franklin, England's greatest Arctic explorer. Franklin *found* the North-West Passage, but at the cost of his own life and that of all the brave men who went with him on his last expedition.

The First Expedition

From boyhood up, Franklin wanted to explore. He joined the Navy when he was fifteen, and fought at the Battle of Trafalgar under Admiral Nelson. He also went on the first expedition that sailed around the coast of Australia.

At the age of thirty, Franklin was asked by the British Admiralty to take up the search for the North-West Passage, at the point where it had been left off by Henry Hudson and William Baffin, 200 years before.

By now something was known about the north coast of Canada, but not much. The Hudson's Bay Company had been organized to trade in furs with the Indians and Eskimos. This Company had built forts and trading-posts in the centre of Canada.

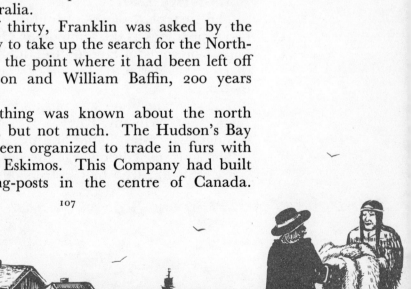

From Prince of Wales' Fort on the shore of Hudson Bay, one of the Company's men, named Samuel Hearne, had gone on foot to explore North-West Canada. He had followed the Coppermine River to the place where it flowed into the Arctic Ocean. He brought back with him maps and a *Journal* of his travels.

Another trader and explorer, Alexander Mackenzie, travelled by canoe down another north-flowing river and reached the Arctic Ocean at a point some way west of the Coppermine. The river explored by Mackenzie was named after him, the Mackenzie River.

Getting Birch-Bark for a canoe

Every summer Company ships sailed through the strait first explored by Hudson, into Hudson Bay. At Prince of Wales Fort and other forts, they took on board cargoes of furs for England. The whole of Hudson Bay had now been explored, and it was known that no opening led out of it into a north-west passage.

However, there was Lancaster Sound, farther to the north, that Baffin had sighted. It led westward, and looked as though it might be the gateway to the North-West Passage.

The first plan of the Admiralty was to send out two expeditions at the same time. One of these would follow the route of Hudson to Hudson Bay, and from there strike overland. The other would travel entirely by sea.

The sea expedition was put under the command of Lieutenant William Parry. He was told to sail through Lancaster Sound and explore beyond it.

The land expedition was in charge of Lieutenant John Franklin, who had instructions to go by sea to

Hardships of Travel in the Barren Lands

the west shore of Hudson Bay. Here he was to land, and lead an expedition overland across the "Barren Lands" of Northern Canada, till he struck the Arctic Ocean. Then he was to work back eastward along the coast. It was hoped that, at some point, he would meet Parry.

This plan was carefully thought out, but it did not succeed. Lieutenant Parry sailed through Lancaster Sound, and discovered some islands. Then he was stopped by pack-ice, and had to turn back.

In 1819 Franklin set out, accompanied by his friend, Dr. Richardson, two naval officers, and one seaman. They travelled as passengers on a ship belonging to the Hudson Bay Company, which landed them at Fort York, one of the Company's forts on the west shore of the Bay.

Eskimo Woman and Child

From Fort York they travelled overland, partly by canoe, partly on foot, nearly 1,000 miles to Fort Providence on Great Slave Lake. On the way they engaged a number of French Canadian boatmen, called *voyageurs*, to paddle and portage their canoes.

At Fort Providence Franklin engaged some Indians to guide him to the Coppermine River, and to hunt for game to feed his party while they travelled. He then pushed on 200 miles farther north, where he spent a winter building a supply base in the wilderness near the source of the Coppermine River. This he called Fort Enterprise.

Franklin knew little about the country, or about the Indians who lived in it. At Fort Enterprise therefore he asked Akaitcho (Big Foot), Chief of the Copper Indians, to lay down a cache of food, to be ready for them at the Fort, on their return journey. In the spring, taking with him his French Canadian

Franklin's first Expedition

boatmen and the rest of the Indian guides and
hunters, he travelled northward down the Coppermine River to its mouth, following Samuel Hearne's
route, and using his map and *Journal* as a guide.

The mouth of the Coppermine, on the Arctic
Ocean, had been the farthest point reached by
Hearne. But for Franklin it was only the starting
point. He and his party of twenty now embarked
in two large canoes and paddled eastward along the
coast. Already, the provisions they had brought with
them were nearly used up, and they had to depend
on fishing and on shooting game. Game on the
"Barren Lands" was often scarce.

They explored and charted 550 miles of the Arctic
coast. At last, at a place they named Point Turnagain,
Franklin realized they were still nowhere near the
mouth of the North-West Passage. Shortage of food
compelled them to turn back and make for their base
at Fort Enterprise. They broke up their canoes, and
went by a short cut overland, marching on foot south-
west across the "Barren Lands". Much of their
baggage had to be left behind.

This journey proved far harder than they had
expected. It was late in the season, and game was
scarce. Soon they had to eat lichen off the rocks.
One by one, the members of the expedition lost their
strength and collapsed on account of scurvy or
starvation.

Franklin now divided his men. He went on with
one group to find the cache of food that was to have
been left at Fort Enterprise. Richardson followed
more slowly with the weaker members of the party.

Franklin reached the Fort—only to find it empty!
He sent the strongest man in his group, Lieutenant
Back, on ahead to look for the Indians. Then he

waited for Richardson.

When the Doctor arrived, he had a terrible tale to tell. One of the Indians in his party, driven crazy by hunger, had attacked and murdered several of the party, including a young naval officer. Richardson had then been forced, in self-defence, to shoot the mad Indian.

Franklin, Richardson, and their men now lay inside Fort Enterprise, too weak to move, and expecting early death from cold and hunger. But, in the meantime, Back had found the Copper Indians. They returned to the Fort, bringing food just in time to save the lives of Franklin, Richardson, and three of their men.

Franklin's first expedition added much to our knowledge of the Arctic. An important part of the Arctic coast had been mapped, and it had been proved that small ships could navigate the sea there.

The Second Expedition

In 1825 Franklin was sent on a second expedition. He was to go overland to the Mackenzie River, and travel down it by canoe to its mouth. Then he was to explore the Arctic coast to the east and west. At the same time a ship commanded by Captain Beechey was to sail around the Alaskan coast, through Bering Strait, and then eastward into the Arctic Ocean. It was hoped that the two expeditions would meet.

Once again, the meeting of land and sea expeditions failed. Captain Beechey's ship was forced by weather conditions to turn back. But Franklin, whose expedition was better planned and outfitted this time, reached the mouth of the Mackenzie. He and his men explored another 1,200 miles of the Arctic coast. When he returned to England with this information,

Franklin's second Expedition

it was possible to make an accurate map of the greater part of Canada's northern coastline.

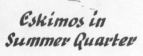

Eskimos in Summer Quarter

However there remained a gap of unknown frozen sea and land extending from Lancaster Sound westward to Point Turnagain, the farthest point eastward reached by Franklin on his first journey along the coast. The sea here was supposed to be full of large islands, but no one knew whether there was a passage through them which would be navigable for ships.

Franklin, who had been knighted by the King for his services, was now sent by the British Government to do important work in other parts of the world. While he was away, Parry, and other explorers, narrowed the gap of the unexplored Arctic coast to a strip of about 500 miles between the Boothia Peninsula and Victoria Island. This region was uninhabited, except for a few Eskimos. It lay frozen under ice and snow nearly all the year. To tell land from sea was hard. Even under the best weather conditions it would be difficult for any ship to make its way through the pack-ice.

The Third Expedition

The British Government decided it was time to solve the riddle, once for all. Sir John Franklin was asked to head a sea-expedition to find out if there really were a passage.

In 1845 he left England with two ships, the *Erebus* and *Terror*, and crews totalling 129 men. The ships were fitted with the best steam-engines available at that time, although a marine-engineer of today would not think highly of them. The men were well-equipped but, although neither the Admiralty nor Franklin realized it, the expedition was too large. As long as

The Erebus and Terror in the Arctic

the men could remain on board they were safe. But should they be forced to abandon ship and take an overland route, it would be difficult to get enough game to feed so many people.

The *Erebus* and *Terror* sailed through Lancaster Sound, past the islands discovered by Parry, and disappeared into the frozen waste. Nothing was heard of them for two years. Then the British Government and people began to worry.

Between 1847 and 1854 one relief expedition after another was sent out to try and find the explorers. All in vain!

In 1854 Dr. John Rae, of the Hudson's Bay Company, travelling overland, found the first clues to their fate. Near King William Island, he met a party of Eskimos who told him of white men who had died of starvation some years before. They produced relics —spoons and forks, coins and knives—that were identified as having belonged to Franklin and his men.

During the next five years these clues were followed up by more search parties. In 1859 the mystery was solved by Captain William McClintock, who had set out in a ship chartered by Sir John Franklin's widow.

This is what had happened.

When the *Erebus* and *Terror* had passed through Lancaster Sound, they ran into a solid wall of pack-ice. This blocked further passage west. They had to find some way around it.

Franklin first tried to pass around the Ice Wall by sailing north-west. But here, too, he found no passage. After spending a winter on Beechey Island, off the coast of Devon Island, he prepared to try sailing in the opposite direction, south-west. In the summer of 1846, when the pack-ice melted somewhat, the ships

Caribou for hungry Eskimos

$1" = 400$ MILES

Franklin's last Voyage

nudged their way along Peel Sound, and through
Franklin Strait. Then they found themselves at a
sort of Arctic crossroads.

Several years earlier Parry had noted that the
northern wall of pack-ice tended to crumble at the
edges in summer. Huge pieces of ice would break
off and drift slowly south-east toward the warmer
water. These pieces were of great size and thickness,
and easily became jammed together in narrow water.
The current carried these floes along the only big
highway open to them, McClintock Channel, and
they drifted on till they came to a sort of bottle-neck.

This bottle-neck was formed by four straits (McClintock, Franklin, James Ross and Victoria) meeting at
one point. Franklin had to guess which of the straits
that faced him (James Ross or Victoria) would *not*
be choked by the ice-floes drifting down from
McClintock Channel.

No one knew, because there were no maps or
charts to guide them. Franklin guessed wrong, and
the expedition entered Victoria Strait. This channel
is frequently blocked by ice all the year round. If
he had chosen the other way (James Ross Strait), he
would have found a passage free of ice in summer.

Before the *Erebus* and *Terror* had gone far down
Victoria Strait, they were caught fast in the ice.
They had to spend a second winter in this position.
Fortunately they had enough food, and the men's
health remained good.

Early in the summer of 1847 Franklin sent out one
of his officers on an overland scouting expedition, to
see where Victoria Strait led.

The officer returned with the news that the frozen
waters of the Strait led on into Simpson Strait, which
had been explored some years earlier from the western
end of the Passage.

N

1" = 400 MILES

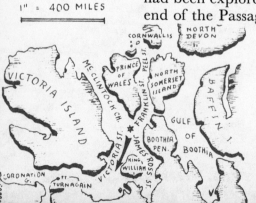

This map shows clearly where Franklin's mistake
led to the death of the entire expedition. Soon
after entering Victoria Strait he was caught in
the ice. If he had tried James Ross Strait he would
have found an open channel, at that time of year.

Now Franklin knew that there really *was* a North-West Passage from the Atlantic to the Arctic Ocean, and so, on to the Pacific Ocean. It only remained for the ships to sail through it.

But the *Erebus* and *Terror* were not fated to be those ships. They were stuck fast in the ice, which never melted at all during that third summer, owing to an unusually cold season. Worse than this, in June 1847 Sir John Franklin, whose health had been broken by his hard life, died.

Captain Crozier now took charge of the expedition.

The summer passed and winter came again—the third winter they had spent in the Arctic, with its long nights and bitter cold. Now food ran short, scurvy broke out, and men began to die.

The fourth summer came. Again the pack-ice did not melt. Captain Crozier was forced by the loss of life and the shortage of food to take a desperate chance.

About 100 officers and men remained. These now left the ships and tried to march south across King William Island to the mainland of Canada. The party was not well equipped for overland travel. They had no dogs to pull their sledges. Their clothing was made of thick wool, which became damp when the men worked and perspired, and then froze when they rested . They did not know how to protect themselves from the cold, as the Eskimos did. They could not catch seals and find game, as the natives did.

Franklin's men never reached their goal. They died, to the last man, on the frozen Arctic wastes. Their bones and equipment were found by McClintock, and by later explorers.

The search for Franklin has been called "the largest man-hunt ever organized". The many expeditions that set out to find him scoured the Arctic lands from end to end. Places that had never before been visited, were now thoroughly explored. Contact was made with the Eskimos, and the white men learned how the Eskimos got their food and kept themselves warm. The Hudson's Bay Company established trading-posts among them.

About fifty years after Franklin found the Passage, Captain Roald Amundsen of Norway guided his ship, the *Gjoa*, through it. It took him two years to complete the voyage with this 72-foot ship, which, although equipped with motor engine, was not heavy enough to force its way through pack-ice.

In 1940–42 Sergeant Larsen of the R.C.M.P. took the *St. Roch*, which had a 150 h.p. diesel engine, all the way from Vancouver to Sydney, Nova Scotia, by this northern route. Later, he made the return journey to Vancouver by the same route.

But not many more ships are likely to use the North-West Passage, on account of the ice. Today it is easier and much quicker to fly over the Arctic wherever one wishes.

However, the "Barren Lands" which Franklin explored have been found to be not so barren, in some ways. They are rich in minerals. Gold, uranium and oil lie under the ice and have been discovered by a new type of explorer—the prospector. No one knows how much additional wealth lies waiting to be discovered.

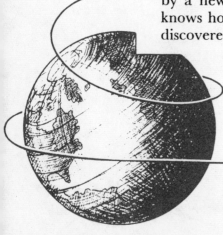

INSIDE AFRICA
HOW IT WAS EXPLORED

A Boer

BRUCE AND ABYSSINIA

LONG after Europe, Asia, and the Americas had been explored, the map of Africa remained almost a complete blank. Only the north coast had been opened up, by traders coming across the Mediterranean Sea.

The Portuguese had sailed around Africa (in the year 1487) to get to India, and had made maps of that part of its coast. Later, the Dutch had settled a colony of "boers" (Dutch for farmers) at the Cape of Good Hope, where the climate was healthy. And many nations, including the British, Portuguese and Arabs, had raided the east and west coasts of Africa, for the cruel purpose of capturing slaves. But the heart of the continent was still a mystery. The mighty rivers of Africa, its natural highways, had not been explored. No one knew the source of the Congo, the Zambesi, the Niger, and the Nile rivers.

From the beginning of history, men had been curious about the Nile. Each year this great river, the second longest in the world, floods its banks for many miles on both sides, laying down a layer of

117

MEDITERR.
SEA

ARABIA

NILE RIVER

RED SEA

ABYSSINIA

LAKE
VICTORIA

:: *Dutch Settlements
at time of Bruce*

::: *Cattle Raising*

ATLANTIC
OCEAN

ZAMBEZI RIVER

MADAGASCAR

ORANGE RIVER

CAPE OF GOOD HOPE

N

INDIAN
OCEAN

1" = 975 MILES

Coffee Plant

fertile mud. When the flood dries up, splendid crops, especially of cotton, are raised on the land. Naturally people wanted to know what caused the flooding, and where the water came from.

Nearly 2,000 years ago, when the Romans ruled Egypt, they explored part way up the Nile. Not far from its mouth they found six cataracts (rapids). Above these cataracts the river flowed through cruel deserts, where sandstorms and hot winds stopped exploration. Later, North Africa was overrun by Arabs and Turks. These people were Mohammedans, and made it almost impossible for Christians from Europe to travel in this region.

But there was one country in East Africa, Abyssinia, that seemed to offer an opening for exploration. Although this country was mountainous and hard to reach, it held an important secret. Somewhere at its heart, so it was said, lay the source of the Nile. The negroes of Abyssinia were Christians, and both the Portuguese and the French had sent missionaries there. But the Abyssinians hated strangers, and either killed the missionaries or drove them away.

The way to Abyssinia lay through either Egypt or Arabia, and both of these countries were controlled by Turks or Arabs. The Arab traders, in particular, did not want Christians to come and trade with the Abyssinians.

But about the year 1700, the people of Western Europe took to drinking coffee. This drink is made from the bean of a plant that grows wild in Abyssinia. The Arabs took this plant to their own country, Arabia (on the Red Sea) and cultivated it. The people of Europe bought their coffee from the Arabs.

The Arabs became accustomed to selling coffee to Christian traders, and so opened the door to Europeans

The Spread of Coffee from Abyssinia throughout the world

who were allowed to visit Egypt and Arabia, and even
to enter Abyssinia. However, the dangers of disease
and robbery, and the differences of language and
religion, kept all but the bravest and strongest from
taking the risk.

James Bruce, a merchant of Scotland, had lost his
wife, whom he loved dearly. To help forget this
sorrow, he turned to travel. He had made friends
with Lord Halifax, the statesman after whom Halifax,
Nova Scotia, is named. It was Lord Halifax who first
suggested a purpose for his travels.

"Why don't you try to find the source of the River
Nile?" he asked Bruce.

Lord Halifax had a reason for suggesting that Bruce
explore the Nile. In 1600 some English merchants
had founded the East India Company, which now
had trading-posts at Madras, Bombay, and Calcutta.
English ships carried metal goods and woollens to
India, and brought home cargoes of calico, silk,
diamonds, tea, and spices.

But it was a long and dangerous voyage to India
around the Cape of Good Hope. The English were
on the look-out for a shorter route. Many people
thought this route might be through the Mediterranean Sea, across Egypt overland, and down the
Red Sea. To explore Abyssinia, and to find the source
of the Nile, might make it easier to open up this route.

Bruce was much interested in the idea of exploring
the Nile. First he took a position with the British
Government in Algiers, on the north coast of Africa.
There he learned Arabic and other Eastern languages,
and picked up some medical knowledge. He also
studied the customs and habits of Eastern peoples.
He learned when to show courage and how to show
tact, and how to win friends among rich and poor

Traders

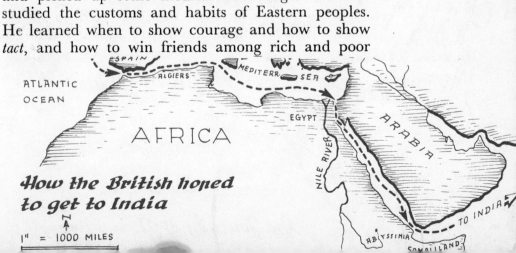

How the British hoped to get to India

people. He also learned how to use scientific instruments, how to draw maps and keep accurate records.

In 1768, Bruce was ready to start for Abyssinia. He had letters of introduction from the rulers of all the leading Arab countries. He sailed slowly up the Nile from its mouth, in a great, two-masted boat with broad sails, stopping to visit and sketch the Pyramids and other wonderful remains of ancient Egypt. Then he came to Assouan, where the cataracts made further sailing impossible. A terrible desert, said to be peopled by robbers, lay ahead of him. He had either to turn back, or find some other way of reaching his goal.

Bruce left the Nile and joined a big caravan of Arab traders and pilgrims that was travelling eastward across the desert to the shores of the Red Sea. There he took ship, and, dressed as a Turkish sailor, travelled slowly along the Arabian coast to Jidda, the port where pilgrims to the holy shrine at Mecca usually land. The heat was frightful, and Bruce was already suffering from sunstroke and fever. However, he made his way to the Turkish Governor of Mecca, showed him his letters of introduction, and secured from him permission to go from Jidda to Massawa. This city was on the western shore of the Red Sea.

Massawa was the only port from which one could enter Abyssinia, but it did not belong to the Abyssinians. The local ruler of Massawa tried to force Bruce to pay him 300 ounces of gold for the right to pass through his city.

"Otherwise," said he, "I will throw you into a dungeon without light, air, or meat, till the bones come through your skin."

Bruce did not have 300 ounces of gold, so he said, as coolly as he could, "Do as you please. But in that

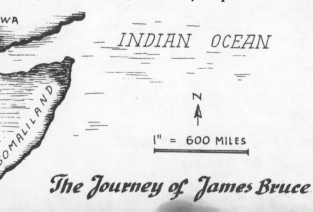

The Journey of James Bruce

case you may expect a visit from an English man-of-war, the *Lion*. I left a message of warning at Jidda, before I came here."

Bruce was not thrown into prison, but was kept waiting at Massawa for two months. Then he was allowed to set out for Gondar, the capital of Abyssinia. Three ranges of mountains lay between him and Gondar. In them lurked savages who hated foreigners.

Hyena

The people of Abyssinia were fighting among themselves. They also suffered from epidemics of smallpox and diseases caused by insects. Slavery and other cruel customs were practised. Bruce recorded all these facts, some of which sounded so strange that people in England refused to believe them. For instance, he said Abyssinians ate steaks of raw meat, which they carved from the backs of living cattle!

Danger cropped up at every stage of his journey. Hyenas attacked his mules, robbers tried to steal his outfit, local rulers threatened him with death or prison. Bruce, who was tall and strong, often saved himself by displaying his skill as a horseman, or as a "dead shot". He possessed a rifle that was far more accurate than the Abyssinian muskets. Sometimes he saved himself by curing the sick.

At last he reached Gondar, a group of 10,000 clay huts perched on top of a flat hill. Here he was lucky enough to win the favour of Esther, the beautiful wife of Abyssinia's chief general, by nursing her son through smallpox. Ras Michael, the general, thought he would like to do Bruce a favour in return.

"Yagoubé (White Man)," he said, "I am told you are a man who makes it his business to wander in solitary places to search for trees and grass, and to sit up all night alone looking at the stars. Our people

Bruce reaches Gondar

are enemies to strangers. If they saw you alone, their first thought would be to murder you. Therefore, to protect you, I have persuaded the King to appoint you Master of his Horse. Go and kiss His Majesty's hands for the favour."

This appointment was not at all to Bruce's liking. It meant he would have to follow the King's army on its campaigns. But he had to do as Ras Michael wished.

The King was so impressed by Bruce's cures of sick people, that he rewarded him by making him owner of the village of Geesh, where the source of the Nile was said to lie. Bruce got a safe-conduct from the King and set out for this place. On the 3rd of November 1770, his guides pointed out to him, from a hill, a tuft of green grass standing in the middle of a marsh. "There," they said, "two springs bubble up. They are the source of the Nile."

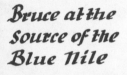

Bruce at the Source of the Blue Nile

"Half-undressed as I was," wrote Bruce in his *Journal,* "and throwing off my shoes, I ran down the hill toward the little island of green sods, about 200 yards distant. The whole side of the hill was thick-grown with flowers, whose bulbous roots gave me two very severe falls. After this I came to the altar of green turf, and stood in rapture over the principal fountain."

Bruce believed he had found the secret of the Nile —its source. But actually he had found only part of it. The Nile is formed of two branches, called from the colour of their waters, the Blue and the White Nile. Bruce had found the source of the Blue Nile.

The snows from the Abyssinian mountains melt each summer and send a flood down the Blue Nile. This joins the White Nile (which is much the longer of the two) at Khartoum. Together they cause the

Nile to overflow its banks in Egypt.

The return journey to Egypt was a nightmare of hardship and dangers. Bruce and his guides had to cross a desert, which was nearly waterless. A suffocating, hot wind blew over it, called the "Simoon." He escaped being buried by sand during a storm, but was hardly able to walk because of an infected foot. He saw many of his companions die of hunger and thirst, and had to leave his instruments and papers behind him. On reaching safety on the banks of the Nile, he insisted at once on getting mules and riding back into the desert to rescue these precious possessions!

On his return, Bruce was praised as a hero by the scientists, but many people said his stories were just "tall tales". Bruce was hurt by these criticisms.

One day he went to dine with some relatives, and heard a guest say it was *impossible* that the Abyssinians could eat raw meat. Bruce left the room and went to the kitchen. Soon he returned, carrying on a plate a piece of raw beefsteak, seasoned with salt and pepper.

"You will eat *that*, Sir, or fight a duel with me!" he cried. When the startled guest had gulped down the raw meat, Bruce added, more calmly, "Now, Sir, you will never again say anything is impossible!"

Bruce thought that if he put his stories in a book, people would be more likely to believe them. Many people read this book and decided that more of Africa should be explored. The African Association was formed to aid exploration of this continent.

The dangers Bruce had met on his journey discouraged the British from starting an overland route to India. But, years later, the Suez Canal was built across the narrowest part of Egypt. Then ships could sail all the way from London, through the Canal, to India.

The Sea Routes to Asia :

The old route ....

The new route – – – – – – – – –

MUNGO PARK AND THE RIVER NIGER

Mungo Park was only twenty-two years old when he applied for a job as explorer.

"I have a passionate desire," he wrote in his letter of application, "to explore some unknown country, and learn about the natives and how they live. I can bear any amount of fatigue. I am young and strong and well able to stand a bad climate."

Mungo was offering his services to the African Association (England), a society which had been formed to encourage men to explore Africa.

At that time the people of England were very upset by the stories that Bruce and others had told them of the cruelties of the African slave-trade. Thousands of negroes were being kidnapped every year by Arab traders, or sold by the native rulers in return for western goods. They were sent down in chain-gangs to the sea coast and shipped (often on British ships) across the Atlantic, to be sold into slavery in America.

The centre of the slave-trade was a stretch of country on the west coast of Africa, near the mouths of two rivers, the Senegal and the Gambia. The Association wanted to find out more about this country, and about the people who lived there. Far inland, it was said, lay a rich city named Timbuktu, which had houses roofed with solid gold. If an explorer could reach this city, he might persuade the native rulers to turn Christian, and sell gold, instead of slaves, to the traders.

Timbuktu, it was known, stood on the banks of a great river, named the Niger. No white man had ever seen the Niger. No one knew where its source

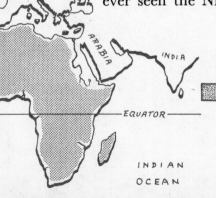

Unknown to Europeans when Mungo Park come to Africa

ATLANTIC OCEAN

EUROPE

ARABIA

INDIA

EQUATOR

INDIAN OCEAN

1" = 300 MILES

was, or in what direction it flowed, or where it reached the sea.

Some people believed it must be a branch of the Nile or the Congo. Others thought the Niger rose in East Africa, flowed west, and then divided into two branches, the Senegal and the Gambia.

To settle this question, the African Association had already sent out an army officer, Major Houghton, to explore the Niger. But before the Major had gone far in Africa, or even set eyes on the Niger, he was attacked by natives and killed. It was not easy to get a man to succeed him, for the salary was small, and the danger very great.

Mungo Park did not care about either of these drawbacks. He had been brought up on a farm in Scotland, and trained to be a medical doctor. But he considered practising medicine at home to be dull work, and longed for a life of adventure, and a chance to add to the world's store of knowledge.

The Association gladly accepted Mungo's offer. In May 1795, he sailed from England to search for the River Niger. He had to find out in which direction it flowed, and to follow its course to the sea.

He chose as his starting point in Africa a small English trading-post named Pisania. This was some distance inland up the Gambia River. Mungo chose Pisania as his starting point for two reasons. First, it was a good place to study the language spoken by most of the natives of those parts. Second, he had been told that the River Niger flowed only a few hundred miles east of Pisania. He hoped to reach the river quickly by an overland march.

Mungo took with him a negro servant, who acted as interpreter, a horse and two asses, a couple of

guns and pistols, an umbrella, a few clothes, some
scientific instruments, and a small collection of
trading-goods, such as beads, amber, and tobacco.
He joined a caravan of slave-traders and travelled
eastward through the steamy jungle. At first all went
well with him, except for a short attack of fever,
which he was able to throw off.

Each district through which Mungo Park had to
pass was ruled by some local chief, who was either a
negro or an Arab. The explorer found he had to
visit each chief in turn, make him a present, get his
permission to cross his land, and secure from him
guides and provisions. Sometimes he was kindly
received, fed, and sent forward. But more often he
was held back, robbed, or ill-treated in some way.

About Christmas time Mungo found himself at the
court of the negro "king" of Bondou. This was the
man who had caused the death of Major Houghton,
so Mungo tried his best to make a good impression.
But when he appeared in his best coat, the King took
a fancy to it, and made Mungo hand it over to him
as a gift. Then, hearing that the white man was
skilled in medicine, he ordered him to visit his ten
wives and look after their health.

The ten black princesses made great fun of Mungo
because of his colour.

"You are white," they told him, "because your
mother bathed you in milk after your birth. Your
nose is very thin. She must have pinched it hard
every day while you were small."

Other negroes were even less polite about Mungo's
skin. They said its whiteness was caused by a hideous
disease. Mungo saw that he looked just as strange
to the black people, on account of his colour, as they
did to him!

The next territory he entered belonged to Ali, an Arab ruler. Ali was a Mohammedan, and disliked Christians. He kept Mungo in close captivity for over a month. He had him stripped, examined, and tormented. Mungo was given little food or water, and became so thirsty that he even drank the muddy water from a cattle-trough. At last he was allowed to continue on his journey, but only after most of his possessions had been taken from him. His interpreter was made one of Ali's slaves. However, he was allowed to keep his horse.

In the next part of his journey, he had trouble from sandstorms, lions, hyenas, mosquitoes, and thirst. But, after many weeks of travelling, he came to a place called Sego, on the banks of the Niger River.

"See the Great Water!" cried a friendly negro who was guiding him. Mungo peered across some marshy ground and spied the object of his travels.

"There was the long-sought-for, majestic Niger," he wrote afterward in his book of *Travels*, "glittering in the morning sun, and flowing slowly *eastward*. I hastened to the brink and, having drunk of the water, lifted up my fervent thanks to the Great Ruler of all things."

Mungo Park thought he had solved the first great riddle—the direction of the Niger's flow. His next task was to follow its course downstream to the sea.

This was more difficult than he had expected. As he travelled eastward along the river bank, the rulers of the villages and towns through which he passed showed themselves unfriendly to white men and Christians. The steamy heat, the insects, and the lack of food brought Mungo down with another attack of fever. At last, at a place called Silla, he

An Arab Chief

N

1" = 660 MILES

SAHARA
DESERT

TIMBUKTU

1795
SENEGAL RIVER
BONDOU
PISANIA
GAMBIA RIVER
SIBIDOOLOO
SEGO
SILLA
NIGER RIVER

GULF OF GUINEA

Park's First Journey

decided he must turn back to Pisania.

But his troubles were not over. Near Sibidooloo, on the south bank of the Niger, he was attacked by brigands, who robbed him of all his remaining clothes except a shirt and a pair of trousers, stole his horse, and broke his pocket-compass. They left him lying almost naked, alone in the desert with lions and hyenas. He was 500 miles from the nearest European settlement. Death stared him in the face.

At this moment nothing but faith in God kept the brave explorer from despair.

A Negro Chief

"I caught sight," he said, "of a small plant of flowering moss, not larger than the top of one of my fingers. At once I thought—can the Being who planted, watered, and brought to perfection this thing of such small importance, look without concern on the sufferings of a creature formed after His own image? Surely not! I started up, disregarding hunger and fatigue, and travelled forward, sure that relief was at hand. I was not disappointed."

Soon after this, Mungo was given food and shelter by a kindly native, who nursed him back to health. The last part of his journey was easier. An Arab slave-trader who was bound for the Gambia River, brought him safely back to Pisania. Mungo had to travel with a gang of slaves who were chained together. But at least he was safe from violence, and had enough to eat and drink.

He reached Pisania after an absence of nineteen months, and soon afterward went home to Scotland. There he wrote the story of his travels, married, and settled down to practise medicine. But after three years, the old restlessness took hold of him.

"I'd rather brave the horrors of Africa," he told

Back in Scotland

a friend, "than ride about these hills visiting one patient after another."

Park's first journey to the Niger was considered so successful that the British Government was willing to send him out again to finish off the work. This time he was given two assistants, five workmen, and a company of thirty-six soldiers, to serve as an escort.

In April 1805, this expedition left Pisania for the Niger, following the route Mungo had used before. But trouble dogged their path from the start. Tropical fevers attacked the soldiers and the workmen, and killed them off like flies. By August, when Mungo reached the Niger once more, he had lost three-quarters of his party! Three months later only four men, besides himself, were still alive.

But Mungo had no thought of turning back. In a letter home he wrote: "I am far from despairing. With the help of one of the soldiers, I have changed a large canoe into a fairly good schooner, on board of which I this day hoisted the British flag. I shall set sail to the East, with the fixed resolution to discover the termination of the Niger, or perish in the attempt."

In this craft, Mungo Park and his companions drifted slowly down the Niger for over 2,000 miles. They passed Timbuktu, a city on the south side of the Sahara Desert. Then the great river began to broaden, and changed its course from north-east to south-east!

The natives who lived on the river bank were often unfriendly to the white men, and tried to rob or attack them. At last one of the native chiefs made up his mind to ambush Park. He placed a small army below the rapids of Boussa, where a great rock nearly blocked the river, and forced the water to flow

Mungo Park

through a narrow gorge. When Park's canoe reached this point, the black men attacked it with lances, pikes, and arrows.

After a brave defence, Park saw there was no chance to get through the ambush. Rather than fall into enemy hands, he jumped overboard, and was drowned. The other white men did the same.

Twenty-one years passed before other explorers, following in Mungo Park's tracks, learned the full story of his death. Then they were astonished to think how nearly he had come to completing his task. He had met death only a few hundred miles north of where the Niger pours its mighty waters into the Atlantic Ocean. However, he had not learned where the Niger started, nor whether it were a separate river from the Congo.

Although many of the negro and Mahommedan chiefs had treated Park cruelly, most of the native people liked him. They felt he was trying to help them. So, by his example, he did much to break down the suspicion the natives had of white people. Now they knew that not all white men meant them harm, as the slave-traders did. Besides this, Mungo Park had proved that it was possible for a white man to travel alone, inland, in the tropical parts of Africa.

African Message Drum

ATLANTIC OCEAN

MADEIRA ISLANDS

CANARY ISLANDS

SAHARA   DESERT

TIMBUKTU

SENEGAL RIVER

Bondou

PISANIA

GAMBIA RIVER

SEGO

SILLA

NIGER RIVER

1805

CENTRAL AFRICA

N

1" = 660 MILES

Park's Second Journey

THE SECRET OF THE NILE

RICHARD BURTON, a young officer in the British Army, wanted to explore the countries of the East. To prepare himself for this task, he learned over thirty languages, including those spoken by the Hindus and Arabs. Then he studied the ways of life and habits of Eastern people (such as the Persians, Hindus, Arabs, Turks) until he could imitate them so well that even a native of one of these countries would mistake him for one of themselves.

His first adventure was a visit to Mecca, in Arabia, the holy city of the Prophet Mohammed. A high wall had been built around this place, and no Christian was allowed in, on pain of death. Burton dressed himself in white garments, pretended to be a pilgrim from a far-off land (Afghanistan, near India), and managed to enter Mecca without being discovered.

Burton's next adventure was to visit Africa, and try to find the source of the White Nile. He had read Bruce's story of his discovery of the Blue Nile. It was now eighty years since Bruce had visited Abyssinia, but the source of the White Nile, the longer branch of the great river, had not yet been found.

Christian missionaries, who had travelled through Abyssinia since the time of Bruce, had brought back tales of a great inland sea lying far to the south. It was surrounded by glittering snow-capped mountains called the "Mountains of the Moon," and here, the White Nile was said to have its beginning. But no white man had ever visited this spot, or even seen these mountains.

Richard Burton persuaded the British Government

Burton, dressed as an Arab

to outfit an expedition for him to lead into that part
of the world. The suggested route would take him
into Somaliland, a small country on the East African
coast, near Abyssinia. Just as he was about to start,
in 1854, he was joined by another young Army officer,
Lieutenant John Speke, a strong, fearless fellow, who
was a dead shot with a rifle.

Burton and Speke landed in Somaliland and, as
they were passing through the country, Burton decided
to make a side-journey into Abyssinia. Speke objected
to this, saying it would make the natives of Somaliland
angry, because they disliked their neighbours, the
Abyssinians.

It turned out that Speke was right. The Somali
attacked their party by night, wounding both Burton
and Speke, and killing an English officer who was
with them. Burton felt he was to blame for this
tragedy, since he was the leader of the expedition.
He began to lose confidence in himself. But Speke,
who had stronger nerves, and whose judgment was
shown to have been better, was not affected by what
had happened. Between the two men, who had been
close friends so far, a little unfriendliness began to
appear. Before long, Burton became jealous of Speke.

The explorers now gave up the idea of travelling
through Somaliland, and followed the coast southward more than 1,000 miles, to Zanzibar. This was
a small island where the Arab slave-traders held their
chief market for the sale of the negroes they captured
on their raids into the interior of Africa.

At Zanzibar they hired Arab guides and negro
porters to carry their supplies. They landed on the
mainland of Africa and struck out due west. First
they crossed a stretch of hot, low-lying coastland,

Waterbuck

MEDITERRANEAN
SEA

EGYPT

ARABIA

NILE RIVER

RED SEA

BLUE NILE

WHITE NILE

ABYSSINIA

SOMALILAND

LAKE
VICTORIA
NYANZA

INDIAN
OCEAN

ZANZIBAR

LAKE
TANGANYIKA

Journey of
Burton and Speke

then they climbed up onto a high plateau that appeared to stretch away, right across Africa. The country was covered with scanty grass and thin forest. Here roamed zebras, antelopes, lions, leopards, and giraffes.

The plateau was broken by a deep ravine, or canyon, running north and south. It had been made by earthquakes centuries ago. Looking down into the canyon, the explorers spied the blue waters of a large lake.

"What is the name of this water?" Burton asked one of his Arab guides.

"It is called by those who live here, Tanganyika."

"And does a large river flow out of it?"

"Yes, Master," said the guide, "at its northern end."

Zebra

Burton was delighted with this news. He felt sure that the river spoken of must be the White Nile. With great difficulty he and Speke made their way by boat to the northern end of the lake. But there they found that their guide had been wrong. There was indeed a river—but it flowed *into*, and not *out of*, Lake Tanganyika. It could not be the White Nile.

This was a bitter disappointment for the explorers. In fact, Burton, who was ill of fever, wanted to give up their search for the White Nile. But Speke pointed toward a range of mountains that lay beyond the lake.

"I am sure," he said, "that those mountains are the 'Land of the Moon', and that we are not far away from the source of the Nile."

Speke begged Burton to let him go on alone to explore, and Burton, who was too ill to accompany him, did not feel he should prevent him from doing so. Then Speke gathered together a new and larger band of guides and porters and set off northward.

He passed through range after range of mountains. Many of these were volcanoes, which rose to 16,000 feet in height, and had caps of snow on their tops. In the deep valleys between the mountains Speke found lakes and small streams, all leading northward. At last he saw an enormous lake that was different from the others. It was so full of islands that it was hard to tell how large it really was. Even beyond the farthest islands, no shoreline could be seen. It was indeed bigger than a lake. It was an inland sea.

"What is it called?" Speke asked his guides.

"Nyanza," they said. "That means Great Water."

"Indeed! Nyanza must be over 100 miles broad. Does any river flow out of it?"

"Yes, Master," came the reply.

"Then we have found the source of the White Nile," declared Speke.

He hurried back to tell Burton of his discovery.

"I intend to call the lake after our gracious Queen Victoria," he said. "Lake Victoria Nyanza."

Burton laughed. "Your lake may be bigger than Lake Tanganyika," he said, "but you have no proof, except what the guide said, that the White Nile flows out of it. You should have explored it to the farther end."

"I am ready to do so," said Speke.

"It is too late now," Burton told him. "We have no more money. We must go back to England."

On the way back to Zanzibar, the men began arguing about whether Lake Tanganyika or Lake Victoria Nyanza were the source of the Nile. By the time they reached Zanzibar, they were bad friends. While Burton stayed in Zanzibar to finish up the business end of the expedition, Speke hurried back to England. There he announced his great

East African Native Weapons

Ripon Falls and Lake Victoria

discovery, and at once asked the Royal Geographical Society to send him out on a second expedition, to settle, once for all, where the White Nile had its source. This the Society agreed to do.

But when Burton arrived in London, he told quite a different tale. He said that Victoria Nyanza was not a lake at all, but a collection of swamps and low hills. He drew a map of Lake Tanganyika, with an imaginary large river flowing out of one end of it.

"This," he said, "must lead on to the source of the White Nile."

However, Burton was too late to prevent Speke from setting out on his second expedition. He took with him, as companion, James Grant, a soldier who wanted to study the plants and flowers of Africa, and draw pictures of them.

Speke and Grant gathered together a huge caravan of Arabs, Hottentots, and Negroes who had been freed from slavery, and started from Zanzibar. They followed the same route that Burton and Speke had used. Soon they reached the country that the natives called the "Land of the Moon". It lay directly south of Lake Victoria Nyanza.

But here they ran into trouble. Many of the Hottentots died of fever. Most of the freed slaves ran away, and Speke found it difficult to get new porters to carry his baggage, food, papers, and instruments. The Arabs were fighting among themselves in the district, and Speke had to act as peacemaker before he could travel any farther.

Now the Arabs told him that there was a second Lake Nyanza, with salty water. It lay to the west of Lake Victoria Nyanza, and it, too, had a river flowing out of it to the north. Speke had not time

An Early Barometer

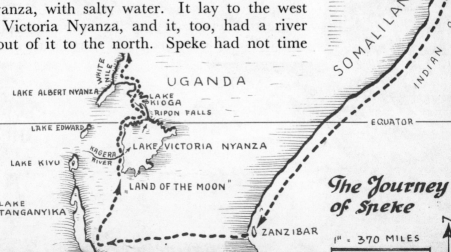

The Journey of Speke

1" = 370 MILES

Hippopotamus

to explore both lakes, so he decided to push on to Lake Victoria Nyanza, and circle its western shore.

Grant had now fallen sick and had to be left behind. Speke reached Lake Victoria Nyanza alone. He was in such a hurry to find the spot where (he felt sure) the White Nile flowed out of the northern end, that he took little trouble to map the coastline of the lake as he went around it. He did not even use a barometer to measure its height above sea level, in order to prove that it was located among high mountains. (This was a mistake, because when he returned to England, he was not able to give satisfactory answers to questions which Burton and other explorers asked him, and many doubted the truth of his account.)

As he travelled around Lake Victoria Nyanza, Speke found himself in Uganda, a country with a rich soil and healthy climate. The people lived mainly on bananas, although fish and game were plentiful. They were ruled by a cruel king, who delighted in making his subjects crawl on their bellies in front of him. Often he had people put to death for very small offences.

Speke won the favour of the King of Uganda, who greatly admired his beard. This was a drawback however, because the King made excuses for keeping the white man with him, hoping that he would tell him how to grow a similar beard. At last Grant, who had recovered from his illness, caught up with Speke, and the two friends were allowed to go on together to search for the source of the White Nile.

In July 1862, Speke's courage and energy were rewarded. He stood by the side of Ripon Falls. Here the head waters of the White Nile pour out of Lake Victoria Nyanza, and start on their 2,000-mile

A Native Ferry

course, northward to the Mediterranean Sea. Speke described the sight in his *Journal*:

"The roar of the water, the thousands of fish leaping up the falls, the native fishermen coming out in boats and standing on the rocks with rod and hook, the hippopotami and crocodiles lying sleepily in the water, the native ferry at work above the falls, and the cattle driven down to drink at the margin of the lake. ... "

Speke was not yet tired of exploring. He decided to follow the White Nile right down from its source to Egypt and the sea. He and his party boarded canoes and paddled downstream for some distance. But then they were stopped by unfriendly natives, and had to continue overland. The farther they went the more difficulties they met with. It took them six months of toil and danger before they reached the native village of Gondekoro. There the Nile leaves the mountains and flows north through the desert.

At Gondekoro, Speke and Grant met another Englishman, Samuel Baker, who had also done much exploring in Africa. Baker had been travelling all the way up the Nile from its mouth to meet Speke, hoping to help him complete his discoveries.

"Is there anything left for me to explore in Uganda?" asked Baker.

"Well," replied Speke, "there is still the lake I did not have time to visit—the second Nyanza. You might like to explore it."

So, while Speke and Grant travelled on down the Nile and went back to England, Baker slowly journeyed *up* the Nile. He first carefully explored the country around the second Nyanza, which he named Albert Nyanza, after Prince Albert, the husband of Queen Victoria. Then he continued to Lake Victoria

Crocodile

Ripon Falls – a series of steep Rapids

Baker's Journey and Explorations

1" = 3000 MILES

N

WHITE NILE

Nyanza. He found that the White Nile started as a little river, fed by mountain streams—the Kagera. This Kagera River flowed into Lake Victoria Nyanza, and from there, by way of Lake Kioga, into the northern end of Lake Albert Nyanza, and out of it again. With this discovery, the course of the Nile River, from its sources to its mouth, was known at last.

Back in England, Burton was still telling people that Speke had been mistaken. The White Nile, he said, flowed, not out of Lake Victoria Nyanza, but out of Lake Tanganyika. When Speke returned, the British Association for the Advancement of Science invited the two explorers to come together at a public meeting and argue their case. Both men accepted, and a large crowd of scientists gathered to hear them.

Burton took his seat on the platform in the hall, next to the vacant chair in which Speke was to sit when he arrived. But Speke never arrived. Instead, a telegram was handed to the chairman of the meeting. It said that, a few hours before, Speke had met his death from an accidental gun-shot, while out shooting partridges on his father's land!

The Burton-Speke debate, of course, did not take place. But when Baker returned to England, the full story was known. Everyone acknowledged that Speke, even if his methods were not always fair, was the true discoverer of the source of the White Nile.

Burton, Speke, Grant, and Baker were interested in exploring for the sake of adding to our knowledge of Africa. One important result of their journeys was the discovery that, although much of Africa was unsuitable for white men to live in, the higher parts of East Africa *were* suitable. Today there are prosperous white communities and large farming areas here.

UGANDA

VICTORIA NILE

LAKE ALBERT NYANZA

LAKE KIOGA

RIPON FALLS

The Source of the White Nile

EQUATOR

LAKE EDWARD

KAGERA RIVER

LAKE VICTORIA NYANZA

LAKE KIVU

LAKE TANGANYIKA

DAVID LIVINGSTONE

WHEN David Livingstone was only ten years old, his parents, who were very poor, took him away from school and sent him to work in a cotton factory. The work was tiring, and the hours were so long that David had little time left to himself. But he was a great reader of books, and had made up his mind to become a medical doctor when he grew up, and heal people's bodies. He attended classes at night after work, and taught himself Latin.

One of the books he read put a fresh idea into his mind. Was it enough to heal people's bodies? Would it not be better to heal their minds also? So David changed his plans and decided that, in addition to practising medicine, he would become a missionary. Missionaries try to help people, particularly those who live in far-off countries, to learn about Christ and accept His Gospel. Of all places, Africa seemed to need most the help of missionaries, because the black peoples were ignorant, savage, and badly treated by slave-traders.

Flamingos

When he had passed his examinations and qualified to be a doctor, David Livingstone offered to work for the London Missionary Society. This Society was anxious to send someone out to East Africa, to persuade the natives there to give up their heathen gods and become Christians.

Livingstone arrived in South East Africa in 1841, and at once set to work. But he soon found it was difficult for a white man to spread the Gospel among the natives, because to most of them the word "white man" meant "slave-trader". For hundreds of years the Portuguese and Arabs had been landing on this

coast, capturing men and women, and selling them for slaves.

At one time, even British ships had helped in this trade, by carrying cargoes of African slaves to the New World. However, by the time Livingstone reached Africa, Britain had seen how cruel and wicked slavery was. English sailors were now forbidden to take part in the slave-trade, and no Englishman might own slaves.

This did not stop the people of other countries from continuing to carry on the trade. The Arabs, who lived in trading settlements on the north-east coast of Africa, made their living by selling black slaves to Portuguese and other slave-dealers. Sometimes a native king would sell his own people to the slavers. Sometimes he would make them pay him heavy taxes in return for a promise not to sell them. Sometimes they paid the Arabs not to capture them. These payments made the natives very poor.

Livingstone had not been long in Africa before he thought of a new way to help the natives. He decided to explore the country inland, and find out which parts had good soil for raising crops and a climate which would be healthy for white people. Then he would try to persuade white farmers and traders to come out and settle in these parts of Africa. From the white men, the natives would learn western ways of living and thinking. In time, they would become Christians of their own free will. He felt sure that the trade in slaves would die out, as soon as the natives had learned to grow their own crops and produce goods of their own which they could exchange for the goods of the people in Western Europe.

But what were the right places for these settlements?

To find this out, Dr. Livingstone travelled on foot, by waggon drawn by oxen, and by canoe, right across Southern Africa, from the east to the west coast and back—in all a distance of over 5,000 miles!

He travelled over rough mountains, along muddy streams, and across the veldt, or open grassland. When he came to a native village, he would stop and teach the native people. He would help them by healing their sick, or by shooting the lions that preyed upon their cattle. Everywhere he won the friendship of the natives by his kindly behaviour. "From nothing that I *say*," he wrote in his diary, "will they learn as much as from what I *am*."

During his journey, he discovered a river, in which lived hippopotami, crocodiles, and flamingoes (great birds with long legs and beaks and bright red feathers). Livingstone's guides told him this river was named "Zambesi", and he explored parts of it by canoe. One day he noticed that the current was becoming dangerously swift. In the distance a mist was rising, and there was a roaring sound like thunder. Livingstone landed and went on through the bush to see what lay ahead.

The Zambesi poured its waters over a mighty waterfall, higher than Niagara Falls. Livingstone was the first white man to see the thrilling sight. He named the falls after Queen Victoria, Victoria Falls.

The discovery of the Zambesi suggested to Livingstone that it might be easier to explore the inland parts of Africa by following the rivers than by striking through the bush on foot. He persuaded the British Government to assist him in preparing for a second expedition, which was to follow the course of the Zambesi and to try to find places for settlements along its banks.

David Livingstone

Livingstone's first Journey

1" = 975 MILES

Livingstone took six years for this task, which proved much harder than he had expected. The Zambesi was full of sandbanks and rapids that made navigation difficult. Also, the natives who lived on its banks were unfriendly. They feared that Dr. Livingstone's explorations would only show the Arab slave-traders the way to reach their country and find their villages! Lastly, the climate was unhealthy, and many of Livingstone's companions on the journey died of tropical illnesses.

He did, however, make one discovery, Lake Nyasa. This lake lay in the centre of high lands suitable for white settlers, and was reached by a river up which boats could travel.

When he returned to England at the end of his Zambesi expedition, Livingstone was fifty-two years of age, and not in good health. But he did not intend to stop working. He wanted to get back to Africa and go on exploring.

While he had been away, Burton and Speke had discovered Lake Tanganyika. Livingstone wanted to explore the country around this lake more carefully than they had done. Perhaps, as Burton had suggested, Lake Tanganyika might be one of the sources of the River Nile. Or it might be the source of another great river, the Congo. He wanted to find out.

Livingstone got help from the British Government and the Royal Geographical Society for this third expedition. He chose for his starting point Zanzibar, an island off the east coast of Africa, where some of his friends lived. He thought these friends would help him to get porters and guides, and would send to him his mail and supplies when he needed them.

But in one way Zanzibar was not a good choice. It was the centre of the Arab slave-trade, which

Zulu Woman

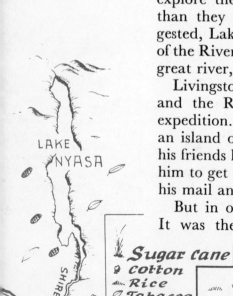

Sugar cane
Cotton
Rice
Tobacco
Cacao

MOZAMBIQUE

The Rich Farming Country
Livingstone Discovered

LAKE
NYASA

SHIRE RIVER

ZAMBESI RIVER

INDIAN OCEAN   1" = 190 MILES

N

Livingstone was doing his best to destroy. **For this** reason, he had many enemies in Zanzibar.

In 1865 he set out with a party of sixty. He planned to visit Lake Nyasa again, and then to work northward to Lake Tanganyika. Two-thirds of the way up the eastern shore of this lake lay the big native village of Ujiji, which Burton and Speke had visited seven years before. Here Livingstone planned to establish a centre for his supplies. It was over 600 miles from the coast, as the crow flies, but he expected his friends would not forget about him and his needs.

Most of the villages through which he passed were empty, because the people had been taken by the slave-traders. Those that remained were starving, and did not want to see any more white men. One by one, the porters whom Livingstone had brought with him from Zanzibar ran away and left him. The animals that carried his baggage died for want of care. But Livingstone pushed on to Lake Nyasa, marched around its southern shore, and started northward, across high bushland to Lake Tanganyika.

Then a terrible blow fell. He had brought along with him two young negroes who had recently been freed from slavery. Livingstone trusted them, and employed one of them to carry his medicine-chest. In it was his supply of quinine, the only drug then known that could cure malaria, a tropical fever carried by mosquitoes. One day both negroes ran away, taking with them part of Livingstone's food—and his medicine-chest!

The Doctor was already ill with malaria, but he pushed on. He believed that he had been sent to Africa by God's will, and that God would protect him while he carried out His work there.

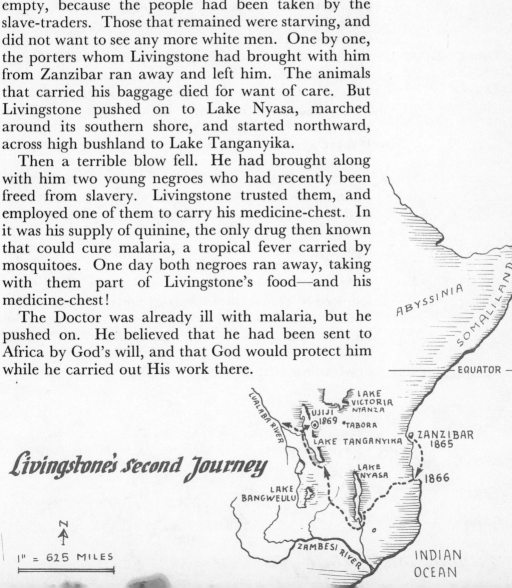

Livingstone's second Journey

N

1" = 625 MILES

Getting Cinchona Bark for Quinine

At last, in the spring of 1869, he reached Ujiji safely. But there he met a great disappointment. There was no mail waiting for him, only a little food, and no medicines—not even quinine. He knew that his friends in Zanzibar could not have forgotten to send these things. The direct route from Zanzibar to Ujiji was shorter than the route he had followed around Lake Nyasa. Therefore, he thought, something must have gone wrong with the supplies on the way.

However, Livingstone did not lose heart. He was sure that his friends would send fresh supplies. In the meantime, he would make a trip westward to explore a mysterious river he had heard of, the Lualaba. This river, he thought, might turn out to be a branch of the Nile.

The Doctor made his journey to the Lualaba during the rainy season. All the streams were flooded, and he had to wade through swamps, swim across swollen rivers, camp in the jungle without proper food or medicines. He suffered from fever and stomach pains. If some friendly Arabs had not helped him, he would have died.

It may seem strange that the Arabs, who were his enemies, should help him. They were the men who were carrying on the slave-trade, so they had no wish to see him succeed in his work. At the same time, knowing what a good and brave man he was, they could not stand by and see him die.

At last Livingstone reached the Lualaba River, and followed its course until it turned north. At this point, illness and lack of food forced him to turn back. If he had been able to follow the Lualaba to the river into which it emptied, and had then followed that river down to the sea, he would have been much surprised

1" = 400 MILES

N

EQUATOR

ATLANTIC

OCEAN

CONGO RIVER

LUALABA RIVER

IUKUGA R.

LUVUA R.

UJIJI

TABORA

LAKE TANGANYIKA

LAKE MWERU

DIED 1873

LAKE BANGWEULU

Livingstone's final Journey

to find it was the mighty Congo!

By promising to repay the Arabs with goods that he expected to find waiting for him at Ujiji, Livingstone got transport for himself and his two faithful negro servants, Susi and Chuma. But when they reached Ujiji again, there were still no supplies. The Doctor was without food, medicine, or money. He had no way of sending for help to Zanzibar. It looked as though he would starve to death.

Of course Livingstone's friends had *not* forgotten to send him supplies and mail, but these had been lost or stolen on the way. One day they noticed some of his porters slinking about the streets of Zanzibar, and questioned them. These porters declared that Livingstone and all his party had been killed by Arabs at Lake Nyasa. They, alone, had returned to tell the tale.

Native Woman of Belgian Congo

A search-party sent out by Livingstone's friends soon learned the truth. Some natives told them that the Doctor was still exploring north of Lake Nyasa. So his friends again sent supplies to Ujiji, thinking they would be there when the Doctor returned to this place. But an Arab porter, who was in charge of bringing the supplies, was not trustworthy. He sold the supplies, and kept the money for himself.

However, help came to Livingstone in a way he did not expect. The newspapers in England, Europe, and America had reported his disappearance in Africa. The owner of a New York newspaper sent one of his assistants to search for Livingstone, and write an exciting story about him for the paper.

This man, Henry Stanley, had never been in Africa, and knew little about exploring. But he did know that Livingstone had last been heard of at Ujiji, so he decided to make for that place.

Stanley went first to Zanzibar. He found it difficult

Livingstone with African Pigmies

to get porters and guides to go inland with him, because cholera, a dreadful stomach disease, had broken out in the city. However, he had plenty of money and, at last, was able to hire six porters who had once served Speke. He also engaged some Indian soldiers to protect him, and bought plenty of supplies. He started for Ujiji in March, with a caravan of nearly 200 men.

Stanley proved to be an excellent leader, and kept his men in order. At one point he had to go far out of his way on account of native wars. At every village through which he passed, the chief made him pay a tax called "hongo", for the right to cross his land. At last, Stanley saw that his stock of trading goods was running low, and made up his mind to pay no more "hongo". For the rest of his journey, he avoided the villages, and led his men through the jungle in dead silence, so that the natives would not hear them.

Because of this, it took him about eight months to reach Ujiji. Livingstone, who did not expect anyone, was sitting in his hut, feeling ill and downhearted.

Suddenly his servant, Susi, ran in crying, "An Englishman, Master! An Englishman!" Then an Arab came in and told him a large caravan was indeed in sight, with bundles of goods, tents, kettles, and food.

At this, Livingstone rose to his feet and walked out to meet the stranger. They met face to face in the market-place, in the middle of a crowd of natives.

"Dr. Livingstone, I presume?" asked Stanley. He was not sure the elderly, grey-haired man he saw, wearing rough clothes, was really Livingstone. But the Doctor reassured him by nodding, and lifting his cap.

"I thank God, Doctor, that I have been permitted

Livingstone, the Teacher

to see you!"

As soon as Stanley's food and medicines had helped Livingstone to get back his strength, the two men took an exploring trip together. Then Stanley urged the Doctor to go back with him to Zanzibar, take ship for England, and have a long holiday before doing any more exploring. But Livingstone would not hear of this.

"If I took a holiday," he said, "I should never come back. First, I must finish my work here."

When the time came for them to part, Livingstone saw his friend off on the road to Zanzibar. "God guide you safe home, and bless you," he said.

Stanley returned to England and America, and told the story of how he had found Livingstone. Later, he returned to Central Africa and became a great explorer there himself.

But for Livingstone there was no return. He went on with the work he felt he had been called by God to complete. He made one more trip from Ujiji, to explore the country south-west of Lake Tanganyika. On this journey he expended the strength he had gained from the food and medicine brought him by Stanley.

One morning his faithful servants found him kneeling by his bedside, as if in prayer. He had died during the night. They carried his body back to Zanzibar. From there it was taken to England, and buried in Westminster Abbey in London.

Only a month after Livingstone's death, the native ruler of Zanzibar did away with the Arab slave-trade in East and Central Africa. This opened the way for missionaries, doctors, and teachers to carry on the good work Livingstone had so bravely begun.

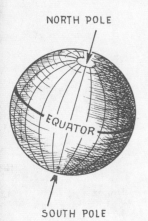

NORTH POLE

EQUATOR

SOUTH POLE

DARING FEATS
OF EXPLORATION

ON TO THE NORTH POLE

FOR 400 years explorers went on trying to reach the North Pole. Why?

The North and South Poles are not real places. They are points at the end of an imaginary line through the centre of the earth, around which it spins as it moves through space. These points are found by making mathematical calculations. There is no land at the North Pole. There is only deep ocean covered with thick ice, which drifts to and fro with the changing seasons of the year.

You cannot live at the North Pole. You cannot even mark the spot where it is, because the surface of the ice there is always shifting its position. There seems little to be gained from being at the North Pole. So it is rather odd that anyone should want to risk his life to get there.

In the early days of exploration, men hoped to find a short cut from Europe to China by sailing north, over the top of the world. They soon found out that the Arctic Ocean was icebound all the year round.

148

EUROPE

NORTH POLE

ARCTIC OCEAN

ARCTIC CIRCLE

ASIA

NORTH AMERICA

BERING SEA

PACIFIC OCEAN

But explorers still tried to sail their ships through the pack-ice as far north as they could. The attempt to get all the way to the Pole by ship was not given up until about 130 years ago.

A new way of reaching the Pole was then attempted. The ship was sailed as far north into the pack-ice as she would go. The explorers landed on the ice, and travelled over it toward the Pole on foot, pulling their baggage on sleighs.

But this kind of travel was difficult and dangerous. Dragging sleighs was back-breaking work. The explorers were tormented by frost-bite and snow-blindness, and were halted by fogs and blizzards. They were never quite sure where they were, because of the drift of the ice. This was not flat and smooth, like the ice in a rink, but piled up in high ridges, with stretches of open water, called "leads", in between.

Eskimo Device for Preventing Snow-Blindness

In spite of these difficulties, about fifty years ago explorers of all countries began racing with each other for the honour of getting "farthest North". The search for the Pole had become a new *kind* of exploration. It was aimed at conquering the earth for the sake of conquest, not for gain. It had become a dangerous, but exciting, game!

This was how Robert Peary, an engineer in the United States Navy, felt when, as a young man, he read about the exploration of Greenland. This aroused his interest in the Arctic, and soon that interest became centred in one thing—the North Pole. As time went on, he began to think about the North Pole almost as if it were an enemy. He had to fight this enemy, and beat it!

Peary was strong, daring, wise, and patient. He

Frozen Arctic Ocean, Showing Leads

bone point

wood

Fish hook

was a good organizer, as well. He saw that the Pole could not be reached in one reckless dash north. The secret of getting there, he decided, lay in careful planning and preparation. He must be like a general carrying through a campaign. He must advance stage by stage, until only the final battle remained to be won.

Peary was lucky in having wealthy friends who helped him to outfit his expeditions, and he took every care to make sure of success. First, he trained himself to live in the Arctic. He became friendly with the Eskimos. He learned how to wear fur clothing and to hunt with spear and harpoon. He ate raw meat and fish. He began to use teams of dogs to draw the sleighs over the ice when he travelled. He learned how to build igloos out of snow when he wanted shelter.

After this, Peary began to consider the best way to reach the North Pole. Greenland was the country that lay farthest north in the Arctic. So Peary carefully explored Northern Greenland. He then established a base at Cape Columbia on Ellesmere Island, the most northerly of the Canadian Arctic islands. Cape Columbia was only 400 miles south of the North Pole.

In some ways, this part of Peary's task was the most difficult. Once he became lost in the darkness of the Arctic mid-winter, and had to have all his toes amputated after being severely frozen. For most men this would have meant an end to their exploring days—but not for Peary.

He now had a ship, the *Roosevelt*, built to his own design. It had wooden sides thirty inches thick, a prow capable of ramming pack-ice, and powerful

Peary's Base-Camp
(see also opposite page)

steam-boilers. In command of this ship was Captain Bob Bartlett, a sturdy Newfoundland sealing-skipper. Bartlett took the *Roosevelt* to within a short distance of Cape Columbia. At this place were gathered over 20 Eskimos and their families with 200 dogs. The northward journey over the ice was ready to start.

In spite of careful planning, this attempt was not successful. Strong gales sprang up. The pack-ice kept shifting, and either piling up into great ridges, or opening into deep cracks with stretches of dark water. The going became worse and worse. Many of the dogs died, and the men suffered from exhaustion and hunger. Peary decided to turn back.

Three years later, in 1908, he was ready to try again. The *Roosevelt* was overhauled and equipped for a fresh voyage. She was again commanded by Bartlett, and had on board twenty-two men, including Matthew Henson, Peary's coloured servant. Henson had accompanied Peary on most of his travels.

Musk-Ox

The ship sailed up the west coast of Greenland to Etah. Here many Eskimos came out in their kayaks to welcome the explorers. Peary took on board fifty of them, with 246 dogs, to go with him on his journey.

Not far from Cape Columbia, the *Roosevelt* was stopped by the pack-ice, and had to be unloaded. Some of her supplies were stored in huts on the shore. The rest were dragged in sleighs over the ice to the base-camp on Cape Columbia.

Besides the supplies they had brought with them, Peary's party secured more meat by shooting game, especially musk-ox. The musk-ox is a short, hairy animal, found only in the Arctic. To protect it from the cold, it has a thick coat partly of fur, partly of wool. The Eskimos used musk-ox skins, not only for making clothes and beds, but also for roofing

Whaling in the Arctic

igloos. From musk-ox bones they made knife handles and tips for their harpoons.

By February 1909 Peary had 24 men, 19 sleighs, and 133 dogs ready for the march over the polar ice. The party was divided into five groups. Four of these were to act as supports for the fifth, which was led by Peary himself. The first four groups were to go ahead, open up a trail, and take food and equipment on to a point less than 150 miles from the North Pole. Then they were to turn back, while Peary's group, which would be fresh, was to make the final dash.

Again the explorers met with bitter cold, biting winds, cracks and gulfs in the ice. One by one, the first four groups finished their part of the task and turned back. By then the expedition had come 280 miles, and was only 133 miles from the Pole.

Peary now took with him Henson, 4 Eskimos, and 38 dogs for his final dash. They made five forced marches over the ice, moving faster than any previous band of Arctic explorers had moved. On the 6th of April 1909 they reached their goal.

"The Pole at last!" wrote Peary in his diary. "The prize of three centuries—mine at last!"

The six men stood in a wilderness of ice, at a point latitude 89° 57′ north, where there is only one direction to look or move—south! Here, every year consists only of one long day and one long night! They stayed at the Pole only thirty hours, making observations of the sun. Then, leaving the flags of the United States and other countries as a marker, they started on their return journey. They had to hurry because the weather was growing warmer, and the "leads" were getting larger every hour.

Peary was successful because he planned his journey

Over the frozen Ocean to the Pole

carefully. He also made good use of Eskimos and their dog-teams. But he had given more thought to reaching the North Pole, than to exploring it. He did not make any study of the conditions of life at the Pole, which would have been useful to scientists. This task was left to later explorers, especially a scientific expedition sent out by Russia in 1927.

These scientists measured the depth of the ocean at the Pole, and found it to be nearly three miles. They examined the plant and animal life in the Polar Sea. They reported on weather conditions. This was particularly useful to aviators who made polar flights.

The first flight to the Pole and back was made from Spitzbergen by Admiral Richard Byrd, of the United States Navy, on the 9th of May 1926. In fifteen hours he had covered the distance which it had taken Peary many months to travel. Two days later Roald Amundsen and Lincoln Ellsworth flew across the Pole from Spitzbergen to Alaska. Two years after that Sir Hubert Wilkins flew across it, in the opposite direction.

In 1932 Sir Hubert also tried to cross the Polar Sea *under* the ice in a submarine, but without success. The submarine that he used was too old and too feeble for the task. This is the only North Pole feat still waiting to be performed by some daring explorer.

The crossing of the Arctic by plane has proved to be more important than the finding of the Pole itself. We now know that bombers can fly direct from Russia to North America across the North Pole—as well as in the opposite direction. If another World War were to break out, it might be fought partly across the Arctic, now thoroughly explored.

Let us hope, however, that the planes which wing their way from continent to continent across the Arctic polar waste will always fly on peaceful missions.

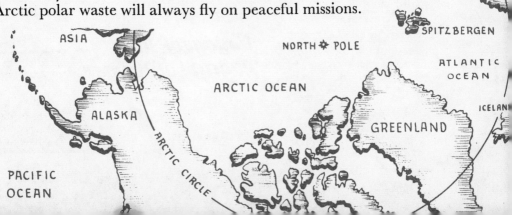

EXPLORING THE ANTARCTIC
(Scott, Shackleton, Byrd)

PEARY had found the North Pole in 1909. Just a year later the South Pole, 12,000 miles away, was reached by men who braved difficulties even greater than Peary had encountered.

Far more interest had been shown in reaching the North Pole than the South Pole, perhaps because navigators had sailed Arctic Seas in search of the North-West Passage. The Southern Seas had been travelled largely in the search for whales, from which oil was made to light lamps before the days of gas and electricity.

On his second voyage, in the *Adventure*, Captain Cook cruised south of the Antarctic Circle in search of a Southern Continent. He did not find it, but that did not prove it was not there. However, for many years after Cook, no further attempts were made to explore the Antarctic.

In 1819, Captain Palmer, of the United States whaling-ship *Hero*, anchored off the South Shetland Islands, about 400 miles south of the tip of South America. Looking southward, he was amazed to see, one clear day, mountains and smoking volcanoes. He had sighted a peninsula, which is now called Graham Land, or sometimes Palmer Land. This is part of the great Southern Continent of Antarctica.

About ten years after this, James Clark Ross, a British explorer, discovered another part of this continent. He sighted a great, white, ice-bound land (1,500 miles due south of New Zealand) and named it "Victoria Land", after Queen Victoria. He explored a deep bay here (Ross Sea), and found two big,

154

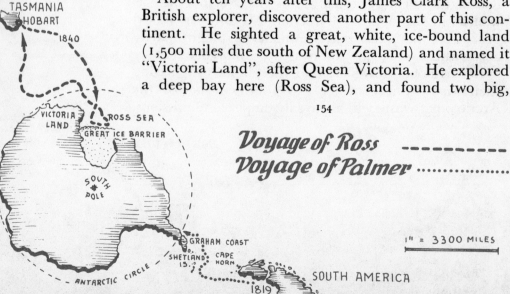

Voyage of Ross — — — — —

Voyage of Palmer ················

1" = 3300 MILES

smoking volcanoes, which he named Mt. Erebus and Mt. Terror, after his two ships.

At last Ross came to a steep cliff of solid ice, nearly 300 feet high. He sailed along it, and thought it might be 1,000 miles long! As it seemed impossible to climb this cliff, Ross named it the Ice Barrier.

The new Antarctic Continent did not look worth exploring. Everywhere there were glaciers, snowy peaks, and icy plains. It appeared to have no inhabitants, and the only living things he saw were penguins and seals. But somewhere in the centre of this continent lay the South Pole. The same desire that had driven men to try to reach the North Pole, now urged them on in a race to reach the South Pole.

In 1901, Robert Falcon Scott, a British naval officer, was sent out to explore the Antarctic. He was given command of the *Discovery*, a ship specially built to withstand stormy seas and crushing ice. He took plenty of equipment and supplies, such as salt pork and biscuit for food, wood for huts, and ponies to pull sleighs. One of his crew was Ernest Shackleton, who later also became a famous explorer.

Scott sailed to the Ross Sea, and explored Victoria Land. He built a hut at the foot of the Ice Barrier, and spent a winter there, looking for some way to climb to the top of it. He believed that the shortest route to the Pole lay directly over this barrier.

To find out what was on the other side of it, he went up in a balloon and looked over the top, just like someone peering over the top of a high wall. He found that the Ice Barrier was not a wall, but a step. From its top the Antarctic Continent stretched in an endless plain of white snow. Blizzards swept its surface, and shaped it into great, frozen waves.

Now Scott realized the difficulties he faced. How could he take supplies up the Ice Barrier? How could his party carry enough food across the frozen plain? There were deep cracks in the ice down which a pony or a man might fall and be lost. But, at least, his course lay entirely across land, which meant that the journey could be made in summer, when the days were at their longest and warmest. This was different from the North Pole, which was in a region of drifting ice, that could be crossed only in mid-winter.

Scott explored the Ice Barrier, and found that the only breaks in it were made by glaciers. With great difficulty, he climbed up one of these glaciers to the top of the Ice Barrier and reached the great plain. Then he and his men travelled southward across the plain for about 300 miles, fighting their way against fierce blizzards. But his men were weak from the two cruel winters they had spent in the Antarctic. Some, including Shackleton, fell ill with scurvy. They were forced to turn back. Next spring the entire expedition returned to England.

Shackleton's Expedition

While Scott was in England getting ready for a second expedition, the search for the South Pole was continued by Shackleton. He bought a whaling-steamer, the *Nimrod*, and sailed to the foot of the Ice Barrier. There he landed, with fifteen sailors and a party of scientists, and spent the winter.

In the spring of 1908, with three companions and sleighs loaded with equipment and drawn by ponies, Shackleton climbed up the glacier to the top of the Ice Barrier. Then began the dangerous journey across the ice-desert to the Pole. It was a long way, 900

miles, and Shackleton was afraid they might not be able to find their way back. He built a number of snow cairns, or mounds, as he went along. They were to serve as signposts for their return journey.

On the 27th of November they passed the farthest point south reached by Scott on his expedition. Then they came to an enormous glacier which Shackleton named "Beardmore". On the way up, three of the ponies slipped on the ice, fell into a crevasse (or crack in the ice), and could not be rescued.

This was a heavy blow. It meant they would have to pull all the sleighs themselves. Also, they would be short of food, for they had planned to kill and eat the ponies when their other provisions were gone.

At the top of Beardmore, they stood on an inner plateau, which Shackleton called the "bleakest and most horrible part of the earth". The plateau was 10,000 feet above the sea, and the air contained so little oxygen it was hard to breathe, when you tried to struggle through the snow. The explorers suffered from headache, snow-blindness, and could hardly pull their sleighs over the humpy surface. Although it was summer, the temperature was often below zero, and the explorers suffered from severe frost-bites. Already their food supply was running low.

At last, although only ninety-seven miles from the Pole, Shackleton had to turn back. He was bitterly disappointed, but felt that his men could no longer endure the gales and blizzards that almost over-whelmed them. This was the 9th of January 1909.

The return march was a race with death. For the last part of it they had no provisions left except tea and cocoa, and one of the party died from stomach pains. The others reached a hut which had been built by Scott on his expedition. They were rescued

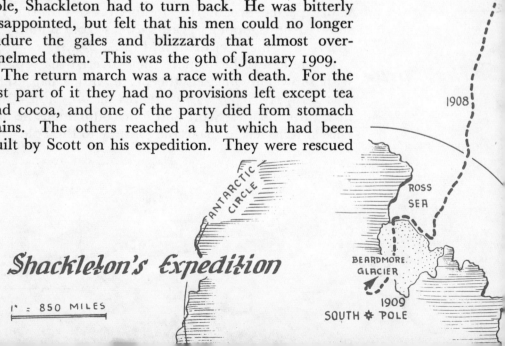

Shackleton's Expedition

1" = 850 MILES

by a landing-party from the *Nimrod*.

Scott's Last Expedition

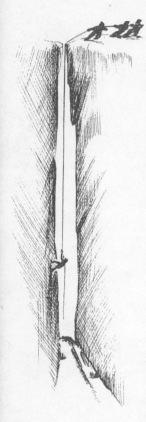

In 1910, Scott set sail in a new ship, the *Terra Nova*, to make a second attempt. His party landed at the foot of the Ice Barrier, where they built huts to live in during the two winters they planned to spend in the Antarctic. The first year was spent in making short expeditions, to prepare them for the final journey.

Scott's plan for reaching the South Pole was like Peary's plan for reaching the North Pole. He divided his men into groups, each of which was to go with him only part of the way, and then turn back. After that, Scott himself, with only a few companions, would make the last dash.

There was need for haste, because they knew that a Norwegian explorer, Amundsen, had made camp not far from them, and would try to beat them to the Pole! The British had an advantage because they had made part of the journey before. On the other hand, Amundsen had a great deal of experience in polar exploration in the North.

Scott and his men first hauled food and equipment up the Ice Barrier and across the plateau to the foot of the Beardmore glacier. They used motor sleighs and ponies for this work. It took longer than they had expected because the motors broke down in the snow. And the ponies grew so weak from pulling the sleighs that many of them had to be shot.

To the Rescue   At the foot of Beardmore they covered the supplies with snow and marked the place with a flag. This was a supply-depot. After it was set up, most of the men turned back. Scott and four companions he had chosen were left to make the journey to the Pole.

On the 4th of January 1912, the little group set out boldly across the inner plateau, facing icy winds and snowstorms. In this wilderness, the snow was so soft that ponies could not be used, and the explorers had to drag their own sleighs. This work exhausted them, but at the end of each day's march they had to make observations with instruments, to make sure they were moving in the right direction.

On the 17th of January Scott and his men reached the South Pole, only to meet disappointment. They found there an empty tent with a Norwegian flag flying above it. Inside was a paper telling them that Amundsen had reached the Pole first!

Amundsen had not won the race just by luck. He had studied Peary's way of travelling in the Arctic, and had learned to use dog-teams, rather than ponies, to pull his sleighs. Dogs were sure-footed. They could shelter in the snow at night, and keep warm. They could cross the wilderness, while the ponies could get no farther than Beardmore glacier.

Making Observations

Also, Amundsen and his men copied the Eskimos in their clothing. The British wore tight-fitting, woollen garments. Amundsen's party ate polar food, such as frozen seal and gull meat. They were not bothered with scurvy. The British learned to do this, but only after making themselves ill by eating too much salted meat, brought from home.

Scott's party began plodding northward on their return journey. The snowstorms were worse than ever, and the men were tired out. One of the party died after a bad fall. The rest struggled on, and reached Beardmore glacier.

Another of the party, Captain Oates, had badly frozen feet. He could not keep up with the march.

They saw the Flag of Norway —
Amundsen had been there first.

Rather than hold back his companions, he staggered out of the tent one night into a blizzard to his death.

Scott and the two remaining men pushed on down the glacier, making shorter marches as they grew weaker. A fierce blizzard halted them for nine whole days! Although they were now only eleven miles from the food-depot, they could not make it. They were too weak to march, and had food left for only two days, and fuel for only one day.

Some time later, rescue parties found the bodies of Scott and his companions. They had kept a full record of their journey, right up to the last.

In England, Scott's *Journal* was published, and read by many people in different parts of the world. The Scott Polar Research Institute was founded at Cambridge University, to keep alive the memory of this great expedition.

After Scott's death, Shackleton took his old ship to the side of Antarctica which is opposite Ross Sea. He hoped to travel right across the continent. But his ship was caught in the pack-ice, and he and his men were rescued with great difficulty.

Admiral Byrd's Flight over the South Pole

Admiral Richard Byrd, of the United States Navy, thought the best way to explore the Antarctic Continent was by plane. He had already flown over the North Pole. In 1928, he led an expedition to the Antarctic, and made ready to fly over the South Pole.

He sailed in a whaling-ship to the foot of the Ice Barrier, and there made a camp which he called "Little America". Here he and his party spent a winter preparing for the trip south by sleigh and plane.

Byrd knew it would be tricky to fly his plane up

The way to the South Pole

Scott's last Expedition -------

Amundsen's Expedition ....

SOUTH AMERICA

over the Ice Barrier, because of the steep downrush of air. However, one clear day in the spring this was accomplished without mishap. The wide Antarctic scene was photographed by special cameras with wide lenses that could take many miles of country on a single film. When these pictures were put together, they could be used to make maps. New mountain ranges were sighted. Equipment and food were dropped to the party toiling along beneath with sleighs, and a supply-depot was set up south of the Beardmore glacier.

Now Byrd was ready for the final dash! The 25th of November brought perfect conditions for the flight. The plane rose over the Ice Barrier, and on to the Pole! Byrd was back at Little America only nineteen hours after taking off! He had flown 1,700 miles without refuelling, which was an unusually long distance for that time.

After this, Byrd and others made flights over the Antarctic Continent. Planes dropped supplies of food and equipment at convenient places, for use by parties of explorers who trudged overland with dog-sleighs. These land explorers did not have to run the risks that Scott, Shackleton, and Amundsen had taken. Aeroplanes and the ability to predict weather conditions accurately had made Antarctic exploration less heroic, but safer. Men were now able to learn and accomplish more without risk of their lives.

Gradually the coastline of the Antarctic Continent was completely explored and mapped. Places were found where the glaciers had melted, leaving lakes and brown, rocky valleys. It is thought that these rocks may contain coal, but no one has yet tried to mine it. Can you suggest why?

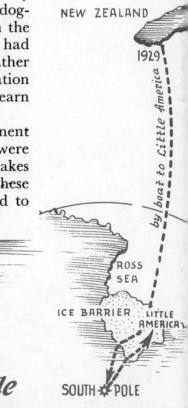

NEW ZEALAND

1929

by boat to Little America

ANTARCTIC CIRCLE

1" = 850 MILES

ROSS SEA

ICE BARRIER   LITTLE AMERICA

SOUTH POLE

Byrd's flight to the South Pole

CLIMBING MOUNT EVEREST

WHAT is there left to explore today on the face of the world? As a look at the map shows, apparently very little. Some tropical jungles in Brazil, some islands in the Pacific Ocean, and some snowy wastes in the Antarctic region. That is all.

But man still has a strong urge to explore. So, in recent years, exploration has taken new forms. It has become a search for places that not long ago were thought hardly worth exploring at all.

Consider the tops of mountains. The highest mountain in the world is Mount Everest in the Himalayas, a range that extends along the north-eastern part of India. Men have learned to calculate the height of a mountain without climbing it. Over a hundred years ago, Everest, which was named after an English surveyor, was found to be at least 29,000 feet high. That is, its top rises nearly five and a half miles above sea level!

It was not until about 1920 that anyone thought seriously of climbing Mount Everest. It stands on the borders of two countries, Tibet and Nepal, into which Europeans were not usually admitted. To the people of Tibet, Everest was a sacred mountain, called in their language "Goddess-Mother of the Earth". They believed that if strangers were allowed there, the goddess would be angry with them.

In 1921, however, the ruler of Tibet gave some British explorers permission to examine the district around Everest, and prepare to climb the mountain. They soon found that the task was going to be very difficult, if not impossible.

The south side of Everest rises in a sheer cliff 15,000

Indian farmer

1" = 900 MILES

feet high. Nothing could be done there.

On the north-east side the only approach is up a long glacier. This leads to a shelf, or ridge, of rock 23,000 feet above sea level. From this ridge it might be possible to climb on to the "shoulder" of Everest, and so reach its top.

But there are only two short periods in the summer each year when climbing on Everest is possible at all. Usually the top peaks are shrouded in cloud or lashed by icy gales and blinding blizzards.

Most important of all, the air above a height of 21,000 feet is very difficult for human beings to breathe. It lacks oxygen. At 28,000 feet the air contains only one-third of the oxygen found at sea level. A climber quickly becomes exhausted at this height. His muscles, his eyesight, and his thinking-power are all affected. It seemed impossible that any ordinary man could scale the last 2,000 feet of Everest.

In the thirty years following 1921, eight expeditions were sent out to try to climb Everest. Each one was made up partly of expert European mountain-climbers, and partly of native Tibetans.

One tribe of Tibetan shepherds, called Sherpas, lives on the lower slopes of Everest. They have lived there a long time, and have developed lungs that can breathe air with less oxygen than the Europeans need. So the Sherpas served as guides and porters for these expeditions.

The European climbers took with them cylinders, or bottles, containing oxygen, which they breathed in at heights over 15,000 feet. This made it possible for them to camp, sleep, and climb on the upper ridges of Mount Everest.

But the weight of the oxygen and cylinders was a

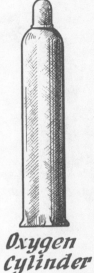

Oxygen Cylinder

drawback. The longer you wanted to breathe it, the more you had to carry. Beyond a certain point, this extra weight cancelled out the advantage received from breathing the oxygen.

Each expedition followed the same plan of operations as that used on Polar expeditions. First, a base-camp was set up about halfway up the side of Everest. Here the explorers lived and kept their supplies.

Pick

From this point, advance-camps were then established at points higher up the mountain. From the last and highest of these camps a team of two or three picked men, who had not used up their strength, but had kept fresh for the job, would make a final dash for the top.

The first expedition, in 1922, had a warning of the dangers of the climb. An avalanche, or fall of snow and rock, crashed down the mountain side without warning and killed seven of the Sherpa porters.

Rope

The second expedition, in 1925, came very near to success. Edward Norton, an experienced climber, managed to reach a height of over 28,000 feet. He was only about 1,000 feet from the top. This acted as a challenge to two younger members of the party, Leigh Mallory and Edward Irvine.

Crampon

On the 7th of June these men set out together to make the final dash. They were last seen through a break in the clouds by a companion who was watching from far below. They were climbing steadily toward the top, with only a few hundred feet to go.

Then the clouds closed in, and they were never seen again. Nearly ten years later the head of an ice-axe was found in the snow, at a point *below* where they had last been seen. It was recognized as belonging to one of the two missing men.

This suggests that Irvine and Mallory may have reached the top of Everest, but either lost their way, or became exhausted while coming down. It is not likely that we shall ever know just what happened.

The next six expeditions succeeded no better than the second. In 1933 two planes, specially designed for the purpose, flew from India and circled over the top of Everest for about fifteen minutes. All the time, they were in danger of being sucked down to death by down-draughts of air around the mountain's peak.

A Sherpa Porter

The following year a British airman lost his life in trying to climb the mountain by himself. It began to look as if Everest might keep its secret for ever.

After World War II, British mountain-climbers prepared for an attack on Everest. By that time Tibet had fallen under Chinese control and could not be used by British explorers for their approach. Nepal, on the other hand, was being opened up. The 1953 expedition attacked the mountain from Nepal on the south side. Then the explorers made their way around to its north-east corner.

The leader of this expedition was Colonel John Hunt, an experienced mountaineer. His task was to *organize* the expedition. He did not try to make the final climb himself. This task was kept for two teams, each made up of two young men, hardened and trained. They were to be kept as fresh as possible up to the last. Then they would be sent ahead to make the final effort.

After great difficulty a base-camp was set up at a height of 15,000 feet. From it a series of eight advance-camps were established. These led, step by step, up to a height of 27,350 feet. The last advance-camp was made on South Col, a saddle-shaped rock joining Everest and a neighbouring peak, Mount Lhotse.

MOUNT EVEREST
SOUTH COL
MOUNT LHOTSE

Tents, sleeping-bags, mattresses, food, cooking equipment, fuel, climbing-gear and oxygen—altogether weighing 500 pounds—had to be carried, with great difficulty, up to this point by the members of the expedition, mainly the Sherpa porters. They used oxygen as little as possible, in order to leave enough for the two teams waiting to make the final try. All this time, the explorers were in a race with the weather. Climbing was possible only in brief intervals between one furious gale or snowstorm and the next.

At last all was ready for the final attempt. It was arranged that each team would make a separate attempt. The first team reached a height of 28,720 feet before being forced by exhaustion to turn back. These men reported that the ridge leading to the top looked very difficult, if not impossible, to climb.

It was now the turn of the second team, made up of Edmund Hillary, a young New Zealand bee-keeper, and Tenzing Norkey, a Sherpa guide. Tenzing had taken part in several of the earlier expeditions.

On the 28th of May, the two men and a group of porters started from South Col, carrying supplies for the final climb. At a height of 27,900 feet, the porters left them to return to South Col, and Hillary and Tenzing made camp. Clearing away snow and pebbles, they fastened their tent down as best they could on a tiny platform of rock about six feet long and six feet wide. After supper they calculated their supply of oxygen. They found they had just enough to see them through.

One side of this platform was overhung by the mountain. The other side fell away in a precipice. Tenzing had to rest that night with his feet hanging over this precipice!

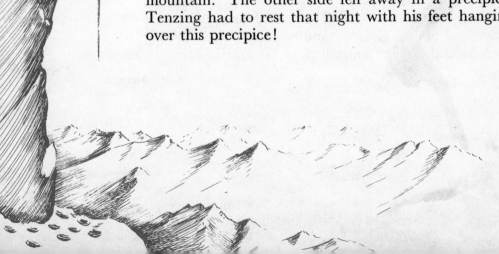

Next morning, in bright sunshine, Hillary and Tenzing began to climb along the last ridge leading to the top. The edge of this was sharp, with a drop of 12,000 feet on one side, and dangerous, jutting shelves of rock on the other. The rock was covered with soft, slippery snow. The climbers were lucky to find two spare bottles of oxygen that had been left for them by the first party, who had made the climb two days earlier.

Hillary and Tenzing roped themselves together. Each took the lead in turn, cutting steps in the frozen snow for the other to follow. They moved slowly, resting after they had gone about forty feet.

In an hour, they reached the foot of a "step" in the rock. This was about forty feet high, and too smooth to scale. They worked their way up a slanting crack in one side of the step. This was the worst part of the ascent.

After two and a half hours, just as they were nearing exhaustion, they found themselves on the top of Everest! They could not speak, because of their oxygen masks. To show their joy they shook hands, and thumped each other on the back. Then they waved flags.

"The whole world around us," said Hillary afterward, "lay spread out like a giant map, and I could take in, with a glance, country we had spent months in exploring."

Hillary took some photographs, while Tenzing buried a small cache of food in a hole in the snow. Then, after only fifteen minutes on the top, the climbers began to feel weak and short of breath. Taking this as a warning not to delay, they lost no time in beginning their downward climb. That night they

slept, weary but triumphant, in the camp at South Col.

The news that Everest had been conquered reached England on the Coronation Day of Queen Elizabeth II of England. She conferred knighthoods on Hillary and Hunt, and a medal on Tenzing.

The success of the climb was due not only to the daring and endurance of the two men who made the last effort, but to the team spirit of the whole expedition, the organizing skill of its leader, and the help given by the scientific equipment with which they had been provided.

Is the climbing of Mount Everest the last feat of exploration to be recorded in man's history? We do not think so.

In recent years, explorers have been going down deep into the earth, searching caves, thousands of feet below its surface. Other explorers have dived toward the bottom of the ocean. Since 1930, the bathysphere, a large, metal globe, with tightly-fitting glass windows, has been in use for deep-diving in order to examine the plant and animal life far down in the sea. In a bathysphere, two French naval officers reached a record depth of 13,287 feet in 1954.

Now that our own planet, the earth, is so nearly all known, some daring scientists are planning to take off in rocket-propelled aircraft, to voyage across space to the moon. Perhaps this dream will become real while you are alive, just as Columbus's dream became real in his time. Who knows?

At any rate, the spirit of adventure which led the explorers of the past, north, south, east, and west across land and sea is alive and vigorous today.

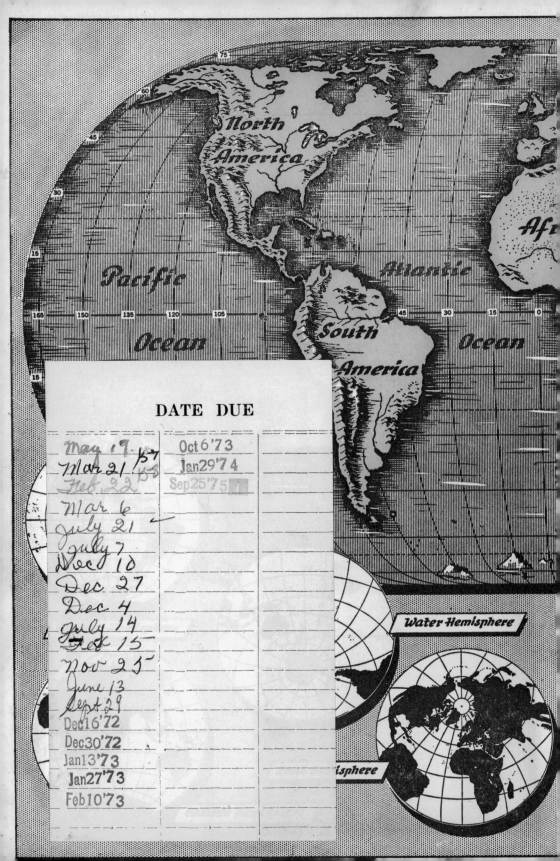

DATE DUE

May 7 '57	Oct 6 '73
Mar 21 '58	Jan 29 '74
Feb 22	Sep 25 '75
Mar 6	
July 21	
July 7	
Dec 10	
Dec 27	
Dec 4	
July 14	
Feb 15	
Nov 25	
June 13	
Sept 29	
Dec 16 '72	
Dec 30 '72	
Jan 13 '73	
Jan 27 '73	
Feb 10 '73	